MORE THAN A MUD FLAP

MORE THAN A MUD FLAP

Raising a Banner of Virtue to the Nations

ANGELA B. BOWLAND

{This book contains explicit content that is inappropriate for innocent eyes and ears.}

DEDICATION

This book is dedicated to my baby sister, Marie. You are and always will be my very, best friend. You have been encouraging me to pursue my dreams our whole lives. Even when I wanted to sell rocks across the cattle guard, you were there to spit shine them for me. When I thought I was a mermaid and swam naked in the icy, cold waters of Grave Creek's irrigation ditch, you stripped and cannon balled in too. When the waves were high and almost overtook me and all others abandoned ship, you were there telling me to hold on. Thank you for believing in me when all others (including myself) didn't and for always being by my side. No one could ever take your place. I bless you with all that God has appointed for you; in this life and the next. I pray that you will walk into eternity with me. "Heaven without you is no place for me, I long to be near you, for always." I love you so much.

~Ace

For I could wish that I myself were cursed and cut off from Christ for the sake of my brothers, those of my own race,

Romans 9:3

ACKNOWLEDGMENTS

I would like to thank and acknowledge the following people;

My Mother-I want to thank you, Mom, for being the rock in our family even when I didn't see you holding us all together. Thank you for being a Mighty Woman of God and always praying for us, girls and your grandchildren. Your prayers have kept me alive when I stepped off the sacred path. Thank you for loving me through those hard years. I understand now what a treasure you truly are. Please forgive me for not noticing sooner. Please forgive me for taking you for granted. I am so proud that you are my Mother. Thank you for being a beautiful example of what a kind, loving, nurturing mother looks like and for always making sure that we were well fed. If I become half the woman you are I will count my life a success.
Thanks, Mom for never giving up on me.
I hope you can see the fruit of your endless labor in my life. I love you so much!

My Children- Autumn Ray, Lalania Vivian-Lynne, Jillian Grace-Marie, and Ethan James you are the reason I live. You are the reason I keep going throughout the hard times. You guys are so incredibly, unconditionally, overwhelmingly loved by me. You guys are the ache in my heart and the sunshine in my day. Autumn in all of your naughtiness and knowledge, Lalania in your defiance and your dance, Jillian in your sweetness and sass and Ethan in your obvious magic tricks and jokes I am so grateful that God has trusted me to be your mother. Thank you for encouraging me to keep believing in my dreams. Thank you for your grace and mercy for all the years I worked on this book. Life without you guys would be so boring! Mommy loves you!

<u>My Dearest Friends</u> —Rebecca, Vanessa, Julie and Alisha where would a girl be without her "sisters"? I am so incredibly blessed to have each and every one of you in my life. I could not imagine life without midnight chocolate runs, warring parties, dancing on 2nd avenue in the light of the high beams, dramas, girly parties, birthday parties, girl's night out, raising children, 5k's, bittersweet marriages and shoulders to cry on. God placed each and every one of you in my life during the most intense times and life has been fully seasoned since. Thank you all for your prayers, encouragement, shared lives, tears, laughter and support throughout our friendships together.
I treasure all of you so very much!

<u>To all others who helped to work on this book</u>; Stephanie McDuffie, Tony Prato, Julie Williams, Tracey Cade, Vanessa Netzloff, Autumn Husek, Storm Steele and Rob Good a huge thank you! To anyone else, I may have forgotten please forgive me and thank you! I could not have gotten this book through the finish line without all of you!

<u>My La Hai Roi;</u> the God who sees me, hears my cries and delivers me from my powerful enemies, I would have died in the desert without You. I can't express the fullness of my gratitude to You here in this short paragraph but you know my heart and the laughter it now brings because of You and Your enduring faithfulness. Thank you for not leaving me broken. Thank you for Your redemption. Without You there wouldn't be a reason for this book.

"If my life is broken when given to Jesus, it is because pieces will feed a multitude, while a loaf will satisfy only a lad."

-Ruth Stull of Peru

CONTENTS

Dedication..4
Acknowledgments......................................5
Part 1:
In The Beginning God Created- The Woman........13
Introduction
    1   Sugar and Spice................................16
    2   A Father's Love..................................28
    3   Eve's Curse...42
    4   Jezebel's Apprentice..........................59

Part 2: Redeeming the Jewels within..................78
Introduction
    5   Tell Me Sweet Little Lies (Venus).....90
    6   Redemption......................................107
    7   True Freedom...................................118

Part 3: Unveiling Our True Identity...................130
Introduction
    8   Battle Scars...135
    9   Treasures In
        Darkness...155
    10 True Love..172

Revolution Virtue...190

To every woman who has ever felt like she was never enough. Make no mistake, for you did not pick this book up by chance. Your Maker has been pursuing you. This is your divine intervention. I call forth a triple hedge of protection around every woman who even handles this book…

With human trafficking being the second largest industry in the United States (next to drug trafficking) I can boldly say America, we have a problem!

Women were not created to be used as sexual objects for mankind. Our value delves so much deeper into the heart of the One who created us. We are the finishing touch to His masterpiece. We are women and yes, we are beautiful but we were created for so much more than to be branded upon a mud flap.

"I pray, Jehovah that Your love and light will shine forth onto all of Your little mud flaps, exposing them to who You created them to be, fully restoring the virtue of Your women."

Amen

WOMEN'S RIGHTS

I am here to **STAND** with you for your rights as a **WOMAN**. You have the right to get your **VALUE** from who you are and not from what you **WEAR**. You have the right to be **EDUCATED**. You have the right to **BE MORE** than skin deep. You have the right to **SPEAK UP** for those who cannot speak for themselves. You have the **RIGHT TO KNOW** that your body is **NOT PUBLIC PROPERTY**. You have the right to know that you are **BEAUTIFUL**. You have the right to cover your breasts (they do not **BELONG** to the wanting eyes of this world). You have the right to **LEAVE** an abusive relationship. You have **EVERY RIGHT TO SAY NO** to forced sex (even from your spouse). You have the **RIGHT** to speak. You have the right to **DANCE** to the beat of your own drum. You have the right to **DRINK**

DEEPLY from this LIFE. You have the right to WALK AWAY. You have the right to be BEAUTIFUL. You have the right to be LOVED. You have the right to SAY NO. You have the right to REVOKE Daisy Duke's rights in your own life. You have the right to be VIRTUOUS. You have the right to RESPECT YOURSELF. You have the right to SET YOUR OWN standards. You have the right to set the STANDARD for your own daughters. You have the right to reclaim your SELF-WORTH. You have the right to be HEALED. You have the right to FIGHT FOR YOUR FREEDOM. You have the right to WALK OFF THE BEATEN PATH and make your own FOOT PRINTS. You have the right to CHANGE THE WORLD.

IN THE BEGINNING

PART 1

GOD CREATED- THE WOMAN

INTRODUCTION

I am going to start by giving you a brief history of my life.

I was born in Ceres, California to a Jerry Wayne and Kathy Ray Davis. I have an older sister, Rebecca and eighteen months after I was born along came my baby sister, Marie (Tracey). My mother got my name off a soap opera. I, of course, know that it was God given. Angela means Angel, which in turn means (heavenly messenger) and I am here today to give you a message of hope in a lost and dying world.

When I was a little girl and still living in California, my grandpa Hamilton would take pictures of my sisters and me. My grandpa was a great fisherman and a great man. He loved his family and wife. He had four beautiful daughters and one son. His wife was the most beautiful woman I have ever known, inside and out. I received her namesake, Beatrice (both of our middle names). My grandfather was the only man in my life that I was ever able to trust. I still remember his smell. He always smelled of Irish Spring soap.

My little sister and I both had light blonde hair (mine straight and hers curly) and my older sister leaned more towards strawberry blonde. We were all really cute in the pictures my grandpa took of us.

I went to the same little, country school in Fortine, Montana all of my grade school years (except for my first time through first grade) in which I had attended Eureka Elementary. That is also where I spent three out of four of my high school years. My freshman year was spent in Anchorage, Alaska.

After high school, I moved to Florida and married my first husband. After three years of living separate in

Florida, we both moved back to Montana and had a second child together. My first husband and I lived together six months off and on, long enough to have my first two children. It was in my second marriage of fifteen plus years that I was refined for Christ. When I speak of my husband I am usually referring to James, my second husband. James and I also had two children together.

One day when I was a grown woman I was sitting in church listening to the special music for that day. As the song played, a sweet vision unfolded before my eyes. I saw ruins, like the ones in Rome. They were strategically placed in a circle and falling down. As I walked through the gate, I saw a lush flower garden with a tree in the middle. I also saw a swing with green vines with white flowers climbing both sides and a little girl about four or five, with long blonde hair, swinging on the swing. "O.K. God, I get the ruins (my life) and the garden (Your life), but who is this little girl?" He spoke to my spirit, "That little girl is you and I'm fixing to restore you back to innocence."

And so my story of restoration began...

1

SUGAR & SPICE

AND THAT'S WHAT MOST LITTLE GIRLS ARE MADE OF

As children, we have all these hopes and dreams of whom and what we will become when we grow up. I wanted to be a pilot, an actress, a mid-evil princess, a singer, a warrior, dressmaker and most of all an explorer. I dreamt of far-off lands in which I would discover ancient artifacts. My mind ran wild with all of the adventures that I would embark upon and the pirate ships that would sail me there? Plenty of my daydreams though were taken captive by the prince who would consume me with his first kiss and conquer me as his own. I made daisy halos and designed the perfect wedding dress for the beginning of our glorious life together.

Year after year I would dream and plan and year after year the leaves would turn crimson and fall leaving only disappointment followed by another lonely winter.

And then one day, I just woke up...

Recently I uncovered an old photograph at my mother's house of me as a newborn, swaddled in bleached, white linens. My dewy, light blonde hair freshly washed peaked over the hospital sheets. I stared at my innocent, little self and just wept. "If only you would have known then what I know now." I wanted to embrace my precious, infant state and warn me of all the times to come but alas it was only a photograph. I held it close to my heart. So, innocent and so pure, looking into my own blue eyes thirty plus years earlier, I longed to protect me from this big, bad world that would have its way with me over and over again. But there's no going back, no returning.

Somewhere on my quest to adulthood reality had robbed me of my childhood hopes and dreams.

But what if the Peter Pan theory didn't always have to come true? What if we could rediscover our youngest hearts and most cherished memories even after we were forced to grow up and leave Neverland?

But is this truly possible?

Come away with me, and we shall embark on this adventure together and by chance, we just may uncover a few lost treasures, perhaps one of them being your heart!

CHILDHOOD ADVENTURES

Growing up we lived on Grave Creek Road, parallel to Grave Creek in Northwestern Montana. The attic that my younger sister (Marie) and I slept in was quite different than the one we have now. The attic we used to sleep in was dark and always hot from the wood stove that our stepdad had installed in the living room below.

The attic had one sheet of plywood covering the 2'x4' walls. You could see above the plywood and below it into the darkness of the attic. Marie and I refused to sleep up there without each other. We used to catch the big pumpkin spiders and put them in lidless canning jars and feed them grass and ants. I vividly remember one cool, summer day sitting in front of the open attic window listening to the rushing water in the creek across the road. Daydreaming, I began to type on the black antique typewriter one index finger at a time. I could smell the freshness of the lilac bushes and the blossoms in my mom's little apple orchard below the second story window. The breeze coming off the cool rain was invigorating. I would sit up there plucking away on that old machine for hours, my imagination running wild. It was very hard to slow down my thought process to suit a two-finger writing speed. I felt like a notorious author.

I would dream about growing up and moving to a big city and writing about all the wild adventures my little sister and I had embark on as children. Like floating down the ditch on big, black inner tubes our stepdad had brought home from the lumber mill. I would write about all those summer days that we had stayed outside all day long building forts and eating freshly ripened raspberries, crisp, green apples, purple plum's, and tart rhubarb but not before dipping every bite into confectioners' sugar. Our mother had a quarter acre garden and planted everything from carrots to cucumbers. We also had a small fruit orchard. During the harvest my mother would pressure cook almost everything that was ripe. Her garden grew onions, carrots, corn on the cob, pumpkins, squash, zucchini and so much more. She made dill pickles and apple pie filling, peach, plum and raspberry jam. Of course, my favorite was her apple butter. No one else in the family liked it so she'd make a batch just for me. I think my favorite time of harvest was when our mother would stay up all hours of the night canning and baking apple turnovers for our sack lunches. My little sister and I would wait until we knew she was sleeping and sneak in and eat as many turnovers as our little stomachs could handle. We definitely woke up to the wooden spoon flying, after those delicious nights.

    My little sister had always been bigger than me, so I called her Chunky Davis. She loathed that name and I got beat up way to many times so I settled on calling her by her middle name "Marie".

    This one time Marie and I told her best friend that we were going to smoke "pot" and we went out to the horse pasture and got a chunk of horse manure, rolled it in toilet paper, stuck toothpaste on the end, lit that puppy up and handed it to Marie's friend!

You don't want to know the outcome of that one!

    And I would not forget about the unbelievable adventure our Uncle Mick sent us on while in Bethel, Alaska. Marie and I (eleven and thirteen at the time) boarded a bush plane in Bethel, with just the pilot, our backpacks and each other and flew seventy seven miles out over the Alaskan tundra and touched down on the Kuskokwim River to spend a week in a bible camp with no running water or electricity, three canvas tents being our only defense against the Alaskan wildlife.

What the heck were our parents thinking!

I still tell my children the stories of when we had snuck out. You have to remember, we lived three miles up Grave Creek Road which was three miles from the nearest highway and then it was at least five miles past that to the nearest general store.
Where in the world were we going? Sneak out and do what?

I often think back to those times, recalling that my childhood was filled with amusement; some of it, however, was so dark, I don't even want to remember it.

For whatever reason, everyone around me used to tell me that I was sexy way before I even knew what that word meant. When we were playing hide and seek, I can't remember hiding without having some boy trying to follow me. Some of them tried to kiss me. When I was 7 or 8, a 10-year old ask me if I wanted to have sex with him and then showed me his parts. I was horrified! For whatever reason, I believe that certain types of girls get thrown into the category of being sexy because of their looks. And, it happens at a very young age.

ADMIRATION

When my youngest daughter was around five years old she was swinging on the swing in our yard. I was standing at the kitchen window watching her long skirt flowing with the sway of the swing. Her long, blonde hair would sweep the ground every time she would lay her head back. As I watched her lovely lips so full and crimson, I thought of how beautiful she truly was. At first, that scared me. Then I heard Gods voice in my spirit, "Why don't you tell her she's beautiful." My first thought was no way because I do not want her to be conceited and shallow. "How could she become conceited and shallow when she doesn't know how truly beautiful she is in the first place?" WOW! I thought. Maybe this is what happens. A mother (or others) sees the beauty her daughter possesses and fears it. Instead, we should embrace it and let her know how beautiful she truly is and compliment her outer beauty and her inner beauty. "That was so beautiful when you got your brother's coat for him." Moms, we have to be aware of this deceitful lie from the enemy. I remember brushing my hair as a little girl and having snide remarks made about how vain I was. How could I have been vain when I had no clue that I was beautiful in the first place, let alone worthy to be fought for?

Little girls want to be admired. And, when we grow up and become big girls, the little girl in us still and will always want to be admired. We want to feel beautiful and cherished, especially when we are pregnant.

Little girls are so much different than little guys; we need admiration. We breathe admiration. We have a deep seeded longing for admiration. Sometimes, we do things that are out of character to get the attention of others. And yes, negative attention is better than no attention.

Allow me to paint a picture in your mind of the girl I had become over time and circumstances. I yearned for whatever kind of attention I could get.

I found that earlier on in my pre-Madonna years (Jr. High), I would do whatever anyone told me I couldn't do. If someone dared me to do something, I was all over it. I loved the glory and the recognition.

Here's an example. One hot, sunny, summer day in the big world of Trego, Montana (population of maybe 200-not counting pigs and chickens), we had moved into Jesse James's trailer park after we had come back from Alaska the second time. We were one of maybe four trailers. On this hot day, my little sister, two of our friends and I were left alone for a few hours (big mistake). We decided to suntan on the roof of our trailer house, saturated with Crisco, cooking oil. Because it was hot, after a while we started smelling like fried chicken. Now, let me explain something to the city folk. When you live in the country, there's not much entertainment. So, we like to make stuff up, the more daring the better.

We were bored and I wanted some glory. Looking around the desolate trailer park with the wild straw grass and the stench of the neighbor's pigs, I saw an old abandoned farm truck. I turned to the other girls, who by now looked like lobsters dipped in butter, and said, "Dare me to go hotwire Old Man James's truck?" They were like "Yeah, right, like you know how to hotwire." So, I jumped off the roof, put my jeans on, and headed over to the truck. I figured old man James didn't have his hearing aids on and would never know. As I got into the truck, I was relieved to see a single key in the ignition. I ducked my head down like I was hotwiring the truck and turned the key over. I pumped the gas pedal to the floor, causing those sunbathing lobsters to come alive. They all jumped off the roof and into the truck. We gathered up our change, headed up to the general store, grabbed a bag of Doritos and a six pack of Pepsi and off we went to the lake. Ah, what a glorious day. I didn't have my driver's license until I was well out of High School, when I "hotwired" Old, Man James's truck, I was probably 16.

During my teen and pre-teen years, there were lots of days when I wanted to be filled with this kind of glory until I felt the consequences, a brief moment of glorification for a lifetime of consequences. I still can't believe that I even entertained some of those dares. Like I said, admiration is what girls want.

ROCK N' ROLL

The music in the late 80's and early 90's played a huge part in my life. The songs spoke to me and guided me, and became laced into my very soul. One time in 6th grade, we had to give an oral report on a song of our choice. If we were brave enough, we could sing the song in front of the class. Some of my girlfriends dared me to sing "Like a Virgin" by Madonna. This was right when this song hit the charts. Of course, I imagined how hilarious that would be, how cool I would look, and how appalled my new teacher would be so I agreed to sing the song. On the day of my oral report, I dressed like Madonna and sang "Like a Virgin" to the whole sixth-grade class, half of whom probably didn't even know what a virgin was. You should know that our school from grades 1 through 8 had about 80 to 83 students. A lot of the parents heard of my performance. I thought it was great. However I had to become known, I would make my mark on the world, as a person, a rebel, or Madonna.

I was also influenced by songs, such as "You are as cold as ice, willing to sacrifice our love." This song actually got into my head and caused me to cheat on my boyfriend at the time. No excuse for that, right. Or, how about the song "Destiny has just been told, my angel, she's a centerfold." Who didn't want to be every mother's nightmare and every schoolboy's dream back then? WOW! Rock N' Roll, no wonder the local church had a secular book and cassette tape burning bonfire. All we heard was that Rock n' Roll was of the devil. "Of the devil, oh that sounds fun, where do I sign up?" This was like a scene straight out of Footloose. That movie reminds me so much of my childhood it's scary.

I cringe to think of how much fun we had with our parents back then. All they were trying to do was save our souls. That's weird. I might have listened if someone would have actually listened to me and just accepted me for me.

Back then, I filled my days with uncanny acts of disgrace, purposely trying to get a response out of my mother; trying to get from her what I needed to feed my inner lion. I honestly just needed her to accept me for who I was and not for whom she thought I should be. I was angry with her for rejecting me.

Deep down I knew it was going to take more than my mother's acceptance to fix me.

That led me to leave home. One of my girlfriends and I loaded everything we had into her little white Mazda 626, and off we went to conquer the world. We were free, so we thought. Yes, free to pay our own bills and buy our own food, which consisted of toast, coffee, and cigarettes. YUM!

We were searching, searching for something or someone to fill this inner hunger, this inner growl, searching for admiration.

Then, we started stealing. Yes, what a rush! Ya that was fun, until we landed ourselves in a jail cell with no creamer for our coffee. OK, we had enough. We proved that we could be as cool as Elvis and do, "the jailhouse rock."

Hey, but those little boards with the numbers on them that we had to hold up after we were arrested really looked cool with our stolen all black apparel. Right!

Man, what were we searching for: recognition, glory? Was I trying to making my ancestors proud? A lot of them were outlaws and I had heard that way back we were actually related to the outlaw Jesse James. Like they'd know how cool we were, THEY WERE DEAD!

Wow! We were like legends in our own minds. And, the music it never helped. It just promoted the delusion, "The wheel in the sky keeps on turning; don't know where I'll be tomorrow." Oh, ya, buddy, how wasteful, how cool, not to care about your tomorrows. Anyhow, why should we care? "Only the good die young." Everyone else grows up and lives an ordinary, mundane existence and never makes the history books.

In some ways, I believe we were all created with this longing, to belong, to be whole, to be loved, to love others, to be recognized as someone irreplaceable. It's universal. "I want you to want me, I need you to need me, and I'd love you to love me," and so on and so on.

Oh, how music impresses these thoughts upon our souls. It reminds us of this great consuming black hole inside of our hearts. Why do we look at movie stars and long to be in their shoes? They're irreplaceable. You could not take a role created for Angelina Jolie and give it to some naive 5'4" farm girl from Fortine, MT. It just wouldn't work. This is what we all long for and this is what we find on the other side of the healing process. We actually find out who we truly are and what role was actually written, specifically for little old me.

We all have things that we go through. There is no way I have enough time to write my life story in its entirety. But, I am no different than you, except perhaps for one thing: My inner self, the depths of my heart have been healed. I have now come back for you. Yes, you are worth my time and energy. My hope is that, through this journey, you will truly see: how precious you are, how fearfully and wonderfully you have been made, how before you were formed in your mother's womb, you were known, and how before you were born, you were set apart and appointed. I have been sent back to spark a hope in you and remind you of the destiny that you have abandoned. Regardless of how you grew up or how others have treated or misplaced you, there is a time and a place for everything under heaven and now is your time for restoration.

2

A FATHER'S LOVE

HOW VITAL IS THE LOVE OF A FATHER?

Incomparable, unfathomable is a father's love. I have read that the father gives his daughter her identity. If little girls do not have this, when these little princesses, ballerinas, and soccer players become young women, to introduce a loving Heavenly Father is almost a joke! Only a select few will be able to see their Heavenly Father for who He truly is and only the ones who seek Him desperately and whole heartedly.

The role of an earthly father is irreplaceable.

I believe this is one way the enemy attacks homes and families. If he can take out the dad this damages the head of the family- all together damaging the family unite that God has designed. This in turn exposes the next generation to spiritual onslaught. I am not saying that God cannot protect a single mother and her children, He will and He does. I am saying that the father is appointed the priest and spiritual head in the home. The family unit is shifted when the father is not present.

The man is spiritually responsible for every family member that God places under him; his wife, children, and any others that have been placed in his permanent care.

So, what happens when a little girl has been raised with an ungodly, unloving, angry or absent father?

Is there any hope for her? Could she ever become a virtuous, righteous woman full of honor, dignity and faith?

If you are one of these little girls, like I was, whose father's love was absent in your life, despair not! All hope is not lost...

Allow me to tell you my story and just maybe you will find hope laced through these pages of my life. Like some of you I was also an abandoned little girl who was separated from my earthly father at a very, young age leaving a tremendous rift in my tender, little soul.

When I was five years old my mother left my father. I remember watching my daddy out of the back window of my Mom's car, while she drove away. I remember thinking," chase me! Fight for me! Come after me!" I remember thinking that I was going to come home from school, in our new home and my daddy would be there. After years of waiting, my daddy never came for me. The lie that I was not worth fighting for became my reality. When we were driving away from my dad, I remember feeling so unprotected. My daddy was my protector and now who would protect me? My Mom used to tell me that my Dad would say that out of all three of us girls (my sisters and I), I was the one he was coming to get. My dad never came. When I was around fourteen years old I was angry at my stepfather and was determined to go find my Dad and live with him. It was around that time that my Mom got the call that my Dad had been killed.

After that, the lie that I was not worth fighting for became my truth. I was not worthy to be loved. My stepdad didn't help me feel worthy. When my Mom married him I was so excited to think that my stepdad could fill the void that my real dad had left behind. I was so wrong about that it wasn't even funny. My stepdad was a hard worker and taught me a lot about being honest and being a "man of your word." He used to say that "you are only as good as your word." I did appreciate the lessons that my stepdad taught me. But most of the time I felt like I was a waste of his time, a burden and just the baggage that came along with the package. A lot of the times, he let his anger get the best of him and my little sister and I were on the other end of his belt. For some reason out of us three girls I was usually the target of his anger. I remember hating him so much that I couldn't even be in the same room with him. Through this time I became very strong willed, extremely rebellious and co-dependent. I also became a fighter. The identity that was impressed upon me was that I was a waste of time; worthless, and unworthy of love. My stepfather was never sexually abusive, but he was very verbally and physically harsh. I also used to blame my Mom for destroying our lives by marrying him and allowing him to treat us that way. We were not deemed precious in any way.

    At times, I was embarrassed to go anywhere because my clothes were dirty and we had the worst hygiene. Don't get me wrong, I had a good mother, who loved me very much. But, I had to put blame for my life somewhere. I know now that my mother did the very best she could in the situation that she was in and I respect her for that. I also appreciate the structure and discipline that I did receive growing up thanks to the choices and sacrifices that my mother and stepdad made for us girls.

    I remember my second year in the first grade when I was voted the ugliest girl in the class. The teacher did not announce it, I read her clipboard. I was always so jealous of the little girl who came in first place as the prettiest. She had the fanciest little, satin dresses and all the other girls would admire her as she twirled around, hair all curled in her shinny little, white shoes. I remember watching her dad drop her off at school and longings rose in my little self that I couldn't explain. I would look down at myself and hope to God that my sox matched and my feet didn't stink. My mother had given me a bowl haircut that year and I remember a little guy with the same haircut asked me if I was a boy or a girl. I asked him what he thought and he said "you're a boy, do you want to play trucks with me?" I was so humiliated I didn't want to go back to school. I couldn't wait to have girls of my own so I could dress them up in pretty, little dresses and buy them the finest ribbons and bows for their hair.

    When I was in seventh grade I got my first kiss. It happened at one of my girlfriend's birthday parties while all of us seventh and eighth graders were running around out in the woods. It was dark, but the moon was full. One of my girlfriends had told me that this really cute guy liked me, but I thought she was joking. There was no way that the second cutest guy in school could possibly like me, but he did. It was getting cold outside and I was running around pretending to hide when this guy found me in the dark and told me that he liked me and bent down and kissed me. I couldn't really see his face because the moon was right behind him. But, I remember feeling like that warm kiss was all a joke and that maybe one of the other guys had dared him to kiss the "ugliest girl in the class." I guess it wasn't a dare. He genuinely liked me. He asked me out and we went out for about a week. Then, I broke up with him because I thought he was making fun of me. I didn't believe I was worthy enough to be attractive to such a hunk of a man. So, I rejected him before he even had a chance to reject me.

One of the deep-seeded issues being separated from my dad caused was the fear of abandonment. This fear was at the core of my being and affected every relationship I was in. Because I had believed the lie that I was not worthy of love, I had major issues loving others. I really didn't know how to have a relationship because I really didn't have a healthy relationship with anyone. I always felt like part of me was missing, unknown and underdeveloped. So, when I started "going out" with boys, even if I thought they were going to dump me I would usually dump them first so I wouldn't have to feel like I was the one being rejected. I would walk away quicker than they could even have a negative feeling about me. This empowered me. I no longer had to be afraid of being rejected when I was the one doing the rejecting. I would take what I wanted from the "relationship" and leave the men in my life wanting. This worked until I got married when I learned the real meaning of commitment. I had no idea how to relate to boys or men. I was never taught how to be in a healthy relationship with a man. Throughout high school and beyond I realized that men only wanted one thing from me and it wasn't conversation. Commitment for me was a tormented prison that I slowly learned to despise. I blamed it on my (Irish), gypsy roots but somehow I knew it stemmed more from my fatherlessness. But this, in my mind, justified my wondering. When I got married I was so afraid that my husband would find out the "truth" about me, think that I was not worthy of being loved, and abandon me. So, every time he was a little bit disappointed I would run away.

After years of trying to run away from my husband and speaking every fear that came into my mind, my worst nightmares came to pass. My husband took his wedding ring off, placed it on the window sill and left me.

After walking through the aftermath of my darkest fears of abandonment, God slowly started to reveal Himself to me as my Heavenly Father. He started to speak to me through His scriptures reassuring me that He would never leave me or forsake me. I didn't trust Him then either. It was through this devastating time that I started to learn how to relate to Him as my Heavenly Father.

Perhaps you too need to know the love and acceptance of a father? Below are a few verses that I clung to through this time.

Can a mother forget the baby at her breast and have no compassion on the child she has borne? Though she may forget, I will not forget you! See, I have engraved you on the palms of my hands;

Isaiah 49:15-

A father to the fatherless, a defender of widows, is God in his holy dwelling.

Psalms 68:5-

Though my father and mother forsake me, the lord will receive me.

Psalms 27:10-

After separating from my biological father I felt I had to protect myself from all onslaughts from my stepdad. His anger would get the best of him and I would stand in defiance feeling like I had to protect my little sister and me against his attacks. I needed to be big and strong in order to withstand his outbursts. During my high school years I got into a lot of fights. Others would pick fights with me but I would release all the built up tension from home upon them. To no avail I had become a scrapper.

When I was 26 I got saved and it was then that my Heavenly Father slowly surrounded me with His love and acceptance.

My stepfather passed away the fall of 2012, leaving me fatherless, again. Even though I was a grown woman with four children of my own somehow that little girl within me felt the burn of abandonment branded upon my heart once more.

On the outside, I looked so fearless. In my heart, I was so afraid; not of the dark or of people physically hurting me, but of my heart being fully exposed.

Through my healing process, it was revealed to me that if I would stop trying to defend myself and lay down that area of my life that God would fight for me and defend me in battle. And so I did. And so He did.

Let me give you an example of His defense as my new Father. I had a really close girlfriend. Our lives were very much braided together in regards to our husband's and children's friendships. She betrayed me in a way that hurt me like I'd never been before. My dearest friend stepped between my husband and I causing a tear in the fiber of my soul. I hadn't felt that separated from love since the day I was forced to leave my daddy. This betrayal went so deep that it separated my heart from my head. I could no longer function the way I used to. My heart was so severely shattered that I knew there was no way all the king's horses and all the kings' men were ever going to put me back together again. The day that I said "I do" was the day I had decided to love and trust a man again. I felt like I had been fooled, hoodwinked. Being loved for me was a joke. My heart had been fully exposed and the lie that I was not worthy of love had become my darkest truth. My emotions were so overwhelming that I could not function normally. God brought me back to the verse on releasing your enemies to Him so he could avenge what they have done (see Romans 12:19&20). I knew if I had tried to take this matter into my own hands, it would have been very messy. I knew that if I had unleashed the rage that was burning inside of me, someone would have been seriously injured and I would have possibly ended up in prison or worse. I refrained and chose to let God avenge me. I released the situation to my Protector. In this matter, I could see the way He was playing chess with my life, so to speak. I could see the way he was moving different ones into town and out. I could actually see Him warring on my behalf. This woman had crossed a forbidden line and met only an angry, jealous Father on the other side. God was contending for me. That reassured me that my God loved me and felt my pain of betrayal. He protected me from the onslaught of the enemy. This woman actually ended up going to prison for years. Honestly after dealing with so much abandonment this situation almost destroyed me, but God used it to reveal His awesome vindication to me. I also found out just how real and active my God truly is. In that darkest hour when I could barely stand, my new Father became my father and loved and defended me ferociously.

There have been many, many more examples of God's protection for me since then. Now I know that I can trust my God to take care of me, to war for me, to avenge me and I also know that He is always with me and will not leave me without defense. I know now how truly precious I am to Him. Now, if anyone hurts me they have to answer to my Heavenly Father. Even though I had to grow up in this life without the love, protection and guidance of an earthly father I feel as though God has redeemed that place in me with His love. I want to encourage all the fatherless girls, you can have a father guide you, defend you, council you, protect you and encourage. How? You ask...honestly just by reading the scriptures and spending time in His presence.

Another thing to consider is allowing an older gentleman to father you. I know sometimes for us girls, who don't know how to relate to men, it's hard to feel comfortable enough to trust a man let alone allow him to father us. But just maybe there will be those brief moments were a father will appear and give us exactly what we need.

Last week my two youngest children and I went to a YWAM seminar. The speaker was talking about The Heart of The Father. My youngest children were not as enthused as I was. We were late so we tried to slip in unnoticed. You know how that works in a small town. Let's just say the speaker stopped talking and invited us to move closer to the group, so much for being incognito.

Considering that the majority of the audiences in the seminar were older more "seasoned" Christians I felt completely out of place and my children asked me if we could leave. Even though I was a little uncomfortable I couldn't seem to get up and go nor did I want to. About a half an hour into this scene I glanced at my children who were sitting one on each side of me. Both of them were listening intently to the speaker completely absorbing, his every word. He spoke with such fatherly love that the inner child in me just wanted to sit on his lap and ask him to tell me stories. I had no idea that I had such a yearning in me to have a "father" speak into my life. I so needed that and so did my children. The speaker had such wisdom and love towards this fatherless generation. After about an hour and half the speaker shifted his focus to prayer and asked anyone if they wanted prayer and so a middle aged couple went to the front. I was not going to voluntarily ask for prayer so I prayed in my head and just told God that if He wanted me to go that someone was going to have to specifically ask me. Sure enough, the couple was done praying and the speaker and his wife looked over at me and my children, "Does anyone else want prayer?" I hesitated and then another woman I knew stood up and turned around to face me and said, "I think we should pray for Angela considering that she is the one with children here." I guess everyone else left their children at home? I didn't get the memo. And so I agreed. I got to the front and the speaker asked me, "Ok, so what would you like prayer for?" and I told him that I wanted to pray for my children that God would restore them from the pain of their father leaving. The speaker looked at me and said," first let's pray for you." Wow, wait a second here, Lord I agreed to allow them to pray for my children. Then the speaker asked me about my father. I told him that I had an angry stepdad and that my mother left my biological father when I was five. Let's just say that within about two minutes I was wrecked, completely undone, weeping, like a little five year old girl. The speaker asked me if he could give me a hug. He smelled so much like my Grandpa Raymond that I just sank into his hug. I didn't want to let go of him and he didn't make me. He allowed me to hug him as long as I needed to. We were both weeping and I just didn't want those hugs to end. For a brief moment in time I was able to experience the human form of a father's love and embrace. I desperately needed that. I was so thankful for this older man who was willing to stand in the gap and just simply hold me. It changed me. Those three hugs were exactly what I needed to seal the fatherly love that my Heavenly Father has been pouring out for the last few years.

    I honestly don't know if men who stand in the "father gap" truly understand how one hug can change everything. In this fatherless generation sometimes, in those moments of abandonment that is all some of us girls need. Simply to be hugged.

    I want to write a public thank you letter to my Heavenly Father for always being there for me when the rest of the men in my life failed to be.

To my Faithful Father,

I want to thank you for rescuing me from the dangers of eternity without You. I want to thank You that You love me so much that You sent Your son to die on my behalf so You could be close to me forever. I want to thank You that when the cares of this world try to pull me under, You are there to carry me. I want to thank You for showing me what real fatherly love looks like. Thank You for getting angry at my enemies when they mess with Your precious, little girl. Thank You that You help me to pay my rent and electricity so that my children will not go without a home. Thank You for caring about my broken heart and helping me put the pieces back together again. What Humpty Dumpty's men and horses failed to do, You did for me. I saw You bend down and scoop up the broken pieces of my mirrored life off the ground and look at me with longing eyes. Thank You for not leaving me broken, but taking every piece of my life and sealing it back together with Your hot glue gun of love. You are my everything and I can't breathe without You. Without You I would be a broken pile of rubbish. Thank You for all the times You have protected me and my children from things I was not even aware of. Thank You for stopping all fiery arrows from the enemy so I could walk on through protected from any danger. Thank You for guiding me and helping me know which path to go down. You are my sweet, sweet Daddy and I love you.

Your precious princess,

Angelina B.B.

3 EVE'S CURSE

SUBMISSION

To the woman, He said, "I will greatly increase your pains in childbearing;

With pain, you will give birth to children. Your desire will be for your husband, and he will rule over you."

Genesis 3:16

May 7th, 2009

Journal-

I hate the curse You put on women! I hate it! I feel like it gives men the opportunity to degrade and demean women and its justified!

This morning I put my water in the microwave for one minute and 20 seconds. My husband sat down on his lunch box to put his work boots on. I asked him if he would pull my water out of the microwave. It was hot and he burnt himself taking it out. He replied, "How long did you put it in for?" I told him and he remarked, "You need to be trained." I was so deeply hurt by this that I lashed out. He told me that I was in a degrading and demeaning position and I said "So, because I am a woman you feel like you have the right to degrade me?" he said "No."

And so this chapter began....

Now, I fully understand why so many women completely turn away from marriage and some from Gods idea of marriage, as I did for a season. No one wants to be controlled or demeaned by any other person and made to feel like lesser of a human.

In my own personal experience, I have found that the men in my life used this "curse" as a way to manipulate me into what they wanted me to do and become and justify their selfishness through scripture! "It's biblical! Women must submit!"

For this very reason, when I was 24 years of age I swore that I was done with all men trying to control me through this ungodly form of submission and rejected the male race altogether.

My stepfather did the best he knew how. I am very grateful for all the lessons that I learned growing up with him. He made me very determined and strong-willed. He taught me how to be a hard worker and not quit just because things were tough. He never told me these things, he showed me through physical discipline. My stepfather never drank or cheated on my Mom, but he had a very bad temper. He ruled with fear and anger and expected my mother and us children to submit to his every whim of outbursts, using scripture to prove that this form of submission was godly.

I grew up with fear and anger laced through my entire being, swearing that I would never allow a man to control me once out of my stepdad's jurisdiction. This was a covenant I made with myself. While I believe that it is not proper for any man or woman to control another person, there needs to be a healthy balance. The atmosphere at my childhood home was mostly hostile.

When I married my second husband, I received Jesus Christ as my Lord and Savior. I hated the word "SUBMIT." To me "submit" meant accepting fear, anger and whatever else your spouse tried to control you with as right and biblical. This form of submission and control repulsed me. I believe that submission is not the power to control, manipulate or demean in any way; not the power to mold or stomp the life, feelings, emotions, ideas or will out of a woman.

This is the negative side, the ungodly idea of submission. It is ungodly because the mind of Christ is not negative and God is love. Wanting to control another person does not portray love. At the beginning of my marriage, I desperately wanted to submit to my husband and follow God's laws. But, every time my husband ruled with fear or anger, I found my childhood flashing through my mind and the vows that I made never to allow any man to control me kept throwing up in my mouth. I found myself fully resisting and rejecting having a man control me through selfishness. I had absolutely no tolerance for this form of submission. It went against everything I was taught in my biblical studies on how to love and honor. It made me want to relate to my husband as I did my stepfather by rejecting all of his authority. My rebellion caused huge strife and confrontation in our family.

I have seen it first hand in myself and other women that this form of manipulation causes little girls to go one of two ways. Either they subconsciously look for a man who resembles their father figure and tries to get out of him all that their father did not give, or they reject men altogether causing open grounds for same-sex relations. I am not saying that this is the way it always works but this is one cause and effect factor that I have witnessed.

The male models in these little girls' lives, however, demand that if women do not obey these rules, then those women are condemned as rebellious and ungodly. This also, in some instances, turns the children away from God, especially the little girls who want so desperately the love and comfort that only a father can give.

"Wives submit to your husbands as to the Lord,"
Ephesians 5: 22.

Is my skin the only skin that crawls when this scripture is read out loud or recited? I can hardly even bear to hear this scripture because it has been so twisted by man. The only thing about "submission" that I just can't accept is when evil spirits work through husbands and the husbands demand that the wives submit to things that do not line up with God's word.

Reading on in that same scripture, one learns that the men are to mirror Christ and love their wives as Christ loved the church. Christ never tries to control anyone.

Here's an example. Suppose your husband demanded that you find another woman to bring into your marriage bed and said that it didn't matter what you thought or said because he was ordained by God to be the head of the house and you were wrong if you did not submit. What would you do? Tell me, is this a form of submission that God ordains or manipulation by man?

I honestly do not believe that the loving God that I serve would tell me to bow down to sin and agree with it? Even accompany it? However, I am called to respect my husband. That is my job regardless of what my husband chooses to do. What does that mean? Does that mean to go along with what he is doing even though you know it is against God? No! God says to come out from among them and be separate (see Isaiah 52:11). Stand up for what is right. God's abundant blessing is on the wife who chooses to follow God's laws, regardless. I would encourage women to stand up for what is right in God's eyes. If you know what your husband is asking you to do does not line up with the laws of God, you have the right and responsibility to stand up and say "No." Some of us were taught as children never to say no to anyone in authority and that we should just "do as we are told."

"Speak up for those who cannot speak for themselves, for the rights of all who are destitute. Speak up and judge fairly; defend the rights of the poor and needy."

Proverbs 31:8

This includes speaking up for our children. I believe that if our husbands are involved in sinful things that threaten to destroy our families, it is our responsibility to our children to stand up for what the scriptures say is right.

If you are reading this book and are recognizing some of the same situations in your own life, get help. If your husband is abusive and controlling, separate yourself from him. God will not condemn you for standing up for what is right and getting away from your husband's sinful behavior until he gets the help he needs. If you're at this point I'd like to recommend a life-changing book written by Dr. James Dobson title Love Must Be Tough. The principles in this book were the exact opposite of what I had been taught growing up yet it is very sound doctrine and biblically based. It changed my way of thinking and challenged me to find my courage and stand up for what was right and just.

Let me ask you something. Is the situation you are in right now glorifying God? If not, I would seriously recommend that you do some soul searching and take an account of your situation. Speak to a counselor, pastor (of the same sex as you), or a godly girlfriend.

It is a grievous form of evil to try to control another person into submission. Think about the relationship we have with God. The Father sent His son to die so we could have an opportunity to CHOOSE eternal life. We have freedom of choice with God. He does not demand or control us into serving Him. He is a God of love and free will. He yearns for us to have a relationship with him but never forces us to.

I had my nine-year-old ask me just the other day, "Why mommy, did God make hell?" "Why does he want people to go to hell?" I told her that God made hell for Satan; He absolutely does not want His children to go to hell. God sent his son to die for our sins so we could go to heaven and be near God forever, but we have to choose God in order to go to heaven. So, God doesn't send people to hell, people send people to hell by not choosing to follow God." God has given us freedom of choice.

We need to remember that yes, God hates divorce and yes we should stay committed to the marriage, if at all possible. God also hates defiled, in your face, sin. Will God hold us accountable for the other partner's sins? No! If we have done all that God has asked us to do in regards to a marriage and our partner has committed adultery and is still in the world, let it be known that God can and has released some from these situations (see Mathew 5:32). We are precious to God. Also, let it be known that God also releases the man from an ungodly, adulterous wife.

This is real and this is life. Yes, we should submit to all of God's ordained authority.

I need to make one thing clear. I am not encouraging women to rebel against those in authority over them, especially if that authority is their husband and he is trying his hardest to follow God and give them and their children a godly foundation. In this case, if the wife chooses to rebel against her husband's authority, she would be in the wrong. The men in our lives are our heads because that is where God has placed them, to love us and protect us. Who are we to stand against them if they are following God? This is a very tender and touchy subject that should ALWAYS be bathed in prayer. I will also encourage you to always, always, ALWAYS follow the leading of the Holy Spirit in this matter. There is no one right answer. Every situation is different and should be treated as so.

We also have to remember that we have a choice to be in the relationship that we are in. Yes, we took a vow before God and to most of us, this is incredibly important. Sadly, the reality of it is, at any point and time our spouse could wake up and proclaim that they do not love us and don't want to be in the marriage anymore. We have to remember that our spouse is choosing to stay in the marriage and get up every day and love us. Appreciate and thank your spouse for that, daily. We cannot treat our spouses anyway that we want and not expect any repercussions. No matter how godly your spouse was raised, after years of constant verbal abuse on your part, they could possibly choose to divorce you. Both parties need to remember that the other party is there by choice. Marriage is not a life sentence, it's a life choice.

FLIP SIDE TO SUBMISSION

Now, we cannot talk about one side of submission and not the other. The other side to submission is the rebellious side. Disrespecting and refusing to submit to anything your husband says. I had a major problem with this side. I truly believe some of it stemmed from not having a voice as a child. Another part was the root of rebellion that I had been harboring.

I remember one morning while doing a bible study God impressed it upon me that I reminded Him of Queen Vashti. For all of you who don't know Queen Vashti, she can be found in the book of Esther under "disrespectful wife." (This is the label that I would give her, anyway)(Esther 1:1-22). Let me tell you my version of the story and then you can read the book of Esther and draw your own conclusion. Queen Vashti had everything most little girls always dream about. She was a queen, she lived in a palace, she had maidservants and someone to cook and clean for her and a hunk of burning love for a husband. Well, one fine day her husband, the King decided to throw a royal banquet and invite all the noblest of men. King Xerxes went all out at this banquet; he had gold and silver couches and jewels in the pavement. Every man there drank from gold goblets and there was an open bar.

In the meantime, Queen Vashti threw her own little powder puff party. On the seventh day, when the king had consumed much wine, he summoned for Queen Vashti to come before him and all of his "well preserved" nobles and show them her beauty.

Queen Vashti was appalled at her husband's request and refused. She was having her own little girly party, anyhow. Queen Vashti knew in her heart that she was more than a trophy wife to be looked upon; however, she greatly disrespected her husband. The king was furious and burned with anger. Why? The king felt incredibly disrespected by his own wife, in front of his own friends, in his OWN home - a big no, no.

So, what does the king do? He takes the advice of his advisors and revokes the Queen's royal position. Not only did Queen Vashti lose her position as the queen that day, she also lost the place in her husband's heart. Oh, to be replaced, by a virgin! Ouch! Some say Vashti was beheaded some say Vashti was banished from the palace but was still taken care of financially. I often wondered if Vashti laid on her wooden bed in her cotton nightgown and watched in anguish as her crown was placed on the head of another woman. She watched as the love of her people was given to another's heart, watched as HER husband took another woman as his wife. I wonder if she thought if only I would have bathed in my oil of myrrh and lathered my finest of lotions on my skin. If only I would have slipped into my softest silks and had one of my maidservants blush my face with make-up and adorn my head with my royal crown. If only I would have taken 20 minutes to go to my king, my husband, then I would be laying on his chest tonight, hearing the sounds of his voice whispering sweet love, to me. I would still be eating those yummy cream tarts, baker Beatrice used to make especially for me. No, but because I chose to disrespect my husband, my heart is torn out watching another woman take my place and give MY husband an heir to my throne, and I am helpless to stop it.

If I was Vashti, I probably would have chosen the beheading.

I honestly know how Vashti felt. God told me this as a warning of the times to come. I was so disrespectful to my husband that I lost the place in his heart. I used to go to his work and crack jokes about him, IN FRONT OF HIM to his co-workers; his own wife disrespecting him in his own work, in front of his own friends – a big no, no. It wasn't until I had lost that place in my husband's heart that I really understood what happened. When another takes your place in your husband's heart, it is almost impossible to knock that "other" person off the throne. It's almost like playing king of the mountain when you were little, only you're dealing with something a little bit more complex, the human heart.

This rebellion ran deep and went way farther back than I even knew. I received a copy of our family history regarding my biological father's side. Let's just say I now understand my random tendencies to become an outlaw. We will dive deeper into the pirate waters another time. But for today let's just call it what it was and that was rebellion. I learned my lesson the hard way with this one.

I serve a God of purity, love, wisdom, and knowledge, a God who never hurts or demeans. When he does correct or convict me, it is for my own good. I have no problem submitting to Gods ways or laws. It's a love thing.

I believe that God's form of submission is when the man mirrors Christ and the woman happily appreciates his protection, love, guidance, leadership, and direction. He leads her through his own personal relationship with God with the help of God's love and guidance. The woman understands that her husband is spiritually responsible for everyone in the family and respects him and helps him raise their children to serve God. When the husband feels like he has heard from God and wants to move to Timbuktu the wife open-mindedly prays with him for clarity and direction. The wife does not allow her emotions to dictate the move. The final decision belongs to the man. Does the wife have a say in whether they move to Timbuktu? Yes, of course, both man and wife should pray together and pray separately about the subject and then if it's God's will they will both have peace. I would seriously suggest praying about every aspect of the situation and completely bathing it in prayer. I think this is how a lot of marital division arises. The husband hears from God on a certain thing and the wife allows her emotions or feelings about it to ruin the beauty and plan God has for them. On the flip side, the husband gets an idea and doesn't take it before the Lord and doesn't consider his wife's feelings and just expects his family to follow him because "he is the head of the house." But, we as women must understand that, whether it is a good idea or a bad idea, the man will stand before God and give an account of the decisions he made for his family. I am not advising you to move away from God and into the world in order to follow your husband (this is unwise as well) (see Mark 10:30 &31). I have had a situation like this in my own life. My husband, four children and I were homeless for a year and a half and stayed with family. God kept impressing it upon my spirit to call out those things that are not as though they are and prophecy for a home (see Romans 4:17). So, I did. The children and I had drawn up blueprints for a house years before. We went all out and it became a castle. One day when I was, once again, disappointed, by not being able to rent yet another house, I drove out to the country. I saw a home that kind of resembled the house the children and I had drawn up. The house was just a shell but had the same features that matched our blueprints. I told my children that, "if that house matches our blueprints and comes up for sale, then I am going to make a faith bid on it." A little while later, the house came up for sale. I called the real estate agent and went to look at it. I was in awe. The house matched the blueprints that the children and I had drawn up, from the walkout basement to the attic where, of course, I would start my business. The only thing that didn't match was the way the stairs cascaded down to the main floor. But, the stairwell was in the right place. (I got the original blueprints from the owners who had built it and in the original blueprints the stairs matched our blueprints). I was so in love with the fact that God saw our blueprints, heard our prayers and had someone else build a house just for us. God kept telling me to prophesy and call this promise forth. In the meantime, my husband and I went to look at a house for rent. Something about the house gave me the willies and I didn't feel right about it. My husband, on the other hand, thought it was great. It was four bedrooms and two bathrooms and two stories. It was definitely big enough, but I really kept feeling that it was the wrong way to go. My husband wouldn't listen to me. We debated over it for about a week. I kept sensing that we needed to stay and pray and within a week or two we would have the house of our blueprints. God impressed it upon me that if we moved to the rental it would be years, if at all, that we would get the house of our dreams. My husband decided to rent the house. We paid for the house and had the keys to the rental house for a half of a week before my husband and children convinced me to move into it. We had been homeless for so long that I felt very selfish for not allowing my family to have a home. I was the only thing standing between my family and their own bedrooms. So, I completely understood their desire to move and the desperation to have our own space. Our children had been sleeping on my mother-in-law's living room floor for a year and a half. I felt in my spirit that renting that house was the wrong thing to do and it would only lead to destruction. It was in a very desolate place. The whole time we were moving in I kept thinking, "We can still get out of this, it's not too late." When we moved into the rental house, I felt we stepped out of the will of God. I knew that if we stepped out of the will of God, He would no longer be obligated to protect or bless us. After we moved into the rental house, we experienced intense fear that caused a lot of really bad things to happen. The cop's had to be called numerous times for violence. We pretty much handed over our marriage and family to the enemy. A little while after that, the house of our blueprints sold. I prayed every day for God to get ALL of us out of the rental house alive, and He did. However, we were incredibly damaged. James and I were not only separated for a year and a half, but we had given up the promise that was waiting for us on the other side of that trial by choosing our flesh over the Holy Spirit. We lived in the rental house for four months before I even felt God's presence. I had to remind myself that He would never leave me or forsake me even though I felt no connection with Him. After that experience, I knew that I never wanted to be separated from God again. The moral of this story is for both partners to pray and listen to God and each other before making decisions because it could cost you your family, your marriage, your promises and perhaps even your life. My advice to every woman is to respect your husband and keep that place in his heart. It is a very sacred place and you want to be the one there. Always remember to treat your husband with respect because he is with you by choice. He chooses to get up and go to work every morning for your family. He chooses to take out the trash and mow the yard. On the flip side, respect yourself and do not bow down or submit to any form of ungodliness. You are no man's slave and in Christ, we are all of equal value.

There is neither Jew nor Greek, slave nor free, male nor female, for you are all one in Christ Jesus.

Galatians 3:28

Always remember that everyone has the freedom to exercise free choice. Above all, submit yourself to God and His ways will hem you in.

4 JEZEBEL'S APPRENTICE

The other day my children and I were walking down the main street and I walked by a secondhand shop. I remembered that there was something that I wanted from the shop, but could not remember what it was. While in the shop my son dropped his bottle out of the stroller. As I bent down to pick it up, something caught my eye on the bookshelf: a tape series entitled *Revive Our Hearts - Become a Woman of Discretion* by *Nancy Leigh Demos*. The first thought that crossed my mind was wow, a teaching that has to do with the heart. I had just discovered that my heart was in need of some repair. I didn't even know if it was a Christian teaching tape or not. It was probably one of those ankle length, wool skirt, crock pot, potluck kind of Christian teachings. The tapes cost $1.25. I only had a $10 bill and really wanted a new skirt and shirt that I saw. I got convicted of putting the tape series back on the wrong isle (trying to rid myself of it) three times. So, I finally just gave in and bought the thing. When we got home that evening, the children were playing outside and I was starting the chili on the stove top when I remembered the ever annoying tape series.

"Play the tape while you're cooking and the children are outside," I heard in my spirit. So, I held my breath and pushed play on the outdated cassette tape. The lady who spoke while I was opening the cans of beans announced that: "Today, Nancy will be teaching about the Proverbs woman." "Oh that's it, I've heard enough, I said to myself. I cannot hear one more sermon on the forever perfect Proverbs 31 woman!" As I was very tempted to run into my bedroom and turn off the tape, Nancy Leigh DeMoss came on and started talking about this adulterous woman in Proverbs who was a Christian woman that did not conduct herself like one, etc. "Oh? Not what I had expected." After I got the pot of chili on, I opened the front door and could smell the fresh, rainy air coming through the screen. I cracked open a Pepsi, filled my glass full of crushed ice and hopped on the kitchen counter able to see my children out the kitchen window from my peak. I put the chili on low, knowing that my husband wouldn't be home until later. I was able to listen to almost half of the teaching on the cool summer day perched on my kitchen counter. I've always wanted to go to New England and for some reason every time I think of maple trees I feel total peace. The more I listened to the tape the more I thought "I'll bet this woman lives in New England in a really cool white house surrounded by maple trees." I looked on the back of the tape case, "Michigan, close enough for comfort." For some reason, that little fact made listening to her so much more pleasant for me. At the end of the series, Nancy told of a woman who, after hearing the tapes, emailed Nancy confessing that she had been a foolish woman and through her foolishness, selfishness, and arrogant, manipulative, ungodly ways had terribly wounded her husband. She had also said that through her ways she had driven her husband to take another man's wife to church. "How could I have driven such a wonderful man to do such a hideous thing before God," this woman's note cried out. Through her brokenness, this woman identified her failure and cried out to God for healing and restoration and God started the process of restoring her.

When I heard the last part of this tape and this other woman's story, everything that Nancy was saying was me. It was like I had written her that email. Mid-way through Nancy reading the letter, I started to cry and realized that I have been a foolish, foolish, woman. I look back now and realize just how foolish I had been. Just like this woman, through my brokenness, I realized all that I had become. As I perched on that counter watching my children through the window, I thought, "By the grace of God I will no longer be a woman whose life leads to death. By the grace of God, I will be a fresh cistern for my beloved husband and all who hear my voice." I realized how deeply I had wounded my husband. I listened to the last part of the series the next afternoon while frying chicken for chicken nachos. After I was done, I inquired of the Lord why He would take such a good man, such as my husband, and place him with a foolish woman, such as me when He knows the future and knew I would hurt him so deeply.

God knew what our life together would look like. I felt deeply for my husband and realized how, through my foolishness, I had terribly wounded him. But I serve a God who loves to restore if we give ourselves to Him.

The most surprising thing about Nancy's teaching was that the adulterous woman was a "Christian woman."

For these commands are a lamp, this teaching is a light, and the corrections of discipline are the way to life, keeping you from the immoral woman, from the smooth tongue of the wayward WIFE (emphasis added).

Proverbs 6:23-24

Do not lust in your heart after her beauty or let her captivate you with her eyes.

Proverbs 6:25

    Let's talk about Jezebel, shall we? Those eyes, that body, those red lips dripping with the blood of the prophets.

    Let's take what we do know about Jezebel and use our imagination for the other parts, shall we? We are going to take a look at the scrolls and I will let you know when my own imagination takes off to be conscious of not adding anything to the scriptures.

    I am giving you the scriptures that go along with what I am saying. Please read the verses for yourself.

So Ahab went home, sullen and angry because Naboth the Jezreelite had said, "I will not give you the inheritance of my fathers." He lay on his bed sulking and refused to eat. His wife Jezebel came in and asked him, "Why are you so sullen? Why won't you eat?" He answered her, "Because I said to Naboth the Jezeerlite, 'Sell me your vineyard; or if you prefer, I will give you another vineyard in its place.' But he said, 'I will not give you my vineyard."

1 King 21:4-6

In 1 Kings 21:4-6, we find out that Jezebel was married to a whiner, Ahab.

Jezebel his wife said, "Is this how you act as king over Israel? Get up and eat! Cheer up. I'll get you the vineyard of Naboth the Jezreelite." So she wrote letters in Ahab's name, placed his seal on them, and sent them to the elders and nobles who lived in Naboth's city with him.

1 Kings 21:7-9

In 1 Kings 21:7-14, we see that no task is too immoral for Jezebel. She was a liar, a thief, and a murderer and had no fear of God. She not only spoke for her husband but also wrote letters in his name and placed his seal upon them. She had full control of the kingdom.

While Jezebel was killing off the Lord's prophets, Obadiah had taken a hundred prophets and hidden them in two caves, fifty in each, and had supplied them with food and water.

1 Kings 18: 4 & 13

And in 1 Kings 18:4 and 13, we see that Jezebel was a prophet killer.

My vision of Jezebel is likened to a cold-hearted sorcerous.

I don't recall the Bible ever saying that Jezebel was beautiful, but we can only imagine that she used every womanly attribute she possessed to get whatever her black heart desired.

Jezebel was born defiled. Her father was Ethbaal, the king and high priest of the Baal worshipping Sidonians (see 1 Kings 16:31).

Baal worship was associated with obsessive sexual acts trying to induce the arousal of the "god of fertility" in order to obtain rain and a good harvest in the land. This worship also included cutting and slashing one's flesh. I haven't researched a lot on Baal worship, but these are a few acts of Baal worship that I did find. I am sure that there were other customs as well (see 1 King 18:28).

Jezebel was born into a legacy where sex was a prerequisite to obtaining a degree in influence and power. This poison laced itself into her very bloodstream. Control through sexual allure. Jezebel didn't so much want to have a bunch of lovers. Her endeavors ran much deeper. Jezebel did not want to be the leader. She wanted to control the leader. She was the woman who led her "king" around by a dog collar with spikes on it. (This is also how I see her.)

Am I trying to glorify this woman? Never! I am trying to expose her ways so that others will recognize her attributes and desire to rid themselves of them the way I had to.

I want you to understand how these "Jezebel traits" influence the men around you.

When a woman operates in the Jezebel style, she destroys good men, great fathers, men after God's own heart. What was Jezebel's main objective besides controlling those around her? Jezebel ordered for the prophets to be killed (see 1 King 18:4). She did not fear God and opted to destroy His people, which is horrifying when you think about her standing before God during the final judgment. No one and nothing is greater than Jehovah, no one. Jezebel was "man", made from the same dust she ate when she hit the ground before Jehu's horses trampled her beautiful wickedness (see 2 Kings 9:30-37).

They should have just thrown a bucket of water on her; I heard this worked for Dorothy in the Wizard of Oz.

Allow me to tell you about the Jezebel traits that were in my life and see if you recognize any of these attributes in your own lives. Some of these traits are so unrecognizable that they have to be pointed out in order to see them. I just thought those characteristics were simply part of who I was.

I had several men in my family life that came and went, like used toilet paper. When their wives were done with them, down the drain they went. Growing up I was around women who slandered the male species often. I had a few cousins who had the naked women on the mud flaps and the calendar girls pinned up in their garages. I felt like this was who I was supposed to be. And, if I could not live up to this standard then I was nothing. I remember wearing provocative clothing at school and before I got home I would change. Marilyn Monroe was my idol. I thought that she was the greatest one to ever captivate the male species. The way she talked, dressed, sang happy birthday to J.F.K., the tragic way that she died. Everyone remembers a woman like Marilyn. I wanted to be captivating.

When I was in high school, I found a vintage swimsuit that looked like it came from Marilyn's era. I wore it all summer. If someone wanted to take my picture, I would bend over and show my cleavage and the half-eye shut, smile. I wanted to be unforgettable.

I remember that after my fourth child was born, I started getting varicose veins. When my big belly was finally gone and I could see my legs again, I noticed these ugly, blue veins and was devastated. I felt like my days as the pin-up girl were over. Who would admire me now? I felt like I was nothing. I had been lied to for so long that I believed that a woman's external features were all that she had. When that was gone, she was worth nothing. This is one of the reasons that I was so devastated when my husband told me that he didn't love me anymore. I thought it had to be because of the stretch marks and varicose veins.

Little did I know that he could care less about such things. It had to do with the condition of my heart.

I had bought into the lie that our looks were all that we had. My goal in life was to walk into a room and have every male in that room want to leave his wife as soon as he laid eyes on me. When James and I first got married, I was still operating this same way. Seven years into our marriage, this lie still existed. He noticed it and would call me on it. I would tell him that he was crazy and that it wasn't MY fault that all men where pigs. I thought the fact that men couldn't control themselves had nothing to do with me. When I would catch a man staring at my cleavage, bare legs etc., I would become disgusted, convincing myself that no man could be trusted. It was kind of a sick, twisted form of revenge for what men had done to me. I know, there is no excuse for causing others to fall, but I did. When James and I would go to an event, I would curl my hair, put my makeup on, and wear something that made me feel powerful and able to control all the little piggies around me. (Please excuse my slang, but this is how I felt). I wanted nothing to do with those men. I just wanted all eyes on me because it made me feel that I still had what it took to be beautiful, captivating, and alluring. I worshiped my body; I felt that they should too. Even after I was saved, this was one of the sins that was so deeply rooted in my being that it was one of the hardest ones to conquer and get rid of. If I didn't have the attention and admiration of men, then what was I? I felt I was nothing but an ugly, old housewife. Not wanting to give in to this stereotype, which was a lie, I kept flirting with other married men. Not that I was an adulterous (in my own mind), but because I was taught that if you don't have the attention of men, then you are nothing. This is one reason my second marriage fell apart. My husband explained this to me years later after fighting, accusing, and finally giving up on me. He told me that when I bent over and allowed others to see down my shirt, what I had was no longer sacred to him. I might as well share it with the whole world.

Another trait that was so prevalent in my life was the power to control stimulated by jealousy and fear. I would use every attribute that I had to try and control my husband into doing whatever I wanted him to do. I would throw fights, throw things, pout, manipulate, or say things in order to get him to do what I wanted. Often I would allure him into the bedroom to keep him from going off with his guy friends. If he wanted to go somewhere and I knew there was going to be a pretty girl there, I would say things and do things to try and get him to not go. I would give ultimatums to my husband. "If you go fishing with the guys, we are so done." Etc. etc., etc. I was incredibly insecure. I thought if I controlled him into doing whatever I wanted, then he wouldn't embarrass me, leave me, or hurt me and I wouldn't lose that control.

Jealousy fueled so many fights. James and I would go to an event and I would scan the room and find the sexiest girl that I could find. I would then turn and watch my husband's eyes and if he so even glanced in her direction, I would immediately accuse him of flirting or knowing her or secretly having an affair with her. I was so incredibly jealous even though I was trying to captivate the attention of every man there. I later learned that this jealousy was rooted in fear, fear of abandonment, fear of not being worthy of love, fear of losing control. I was so afraid of not being enough. Not pretty enough, not smart enough, not worthy enough.

I had a lot of vanities. I wasn't just vain. I had become, in my own eyes, completely hollow. I was empty, hollow, without worth. I believed my outward appearance was all I had because my inside was so messed up.

I had become my husband's puppet master. One day he just got tired of being on strings and cut loose. It was through this time that I sought deliverance from operating under my deceiving traits. It's incredibly sobering what people will do when they finally realize that they are losing control over a situation or a person. I became a person I thought I would never become. I did things I thought that I would never do. I believed lies and I lied. I would say and do anything to try and gain the control back that I had over my husband.

After my fourth child was born, I began to lose a lot of weight. I would go to the lakes and rivers with my four children and completely flaunt my body. I would wear a swimsuit top (of course white-resembling M. Monroe) and a pair of cut off shorts. My shorts would cover my varicose veins and my stretch marks were below my belly button. The one thought that kept coming over and over in my head was: I look so good for having four children. And, I would just flaunt it, especially if an ex-boyfriend or a man I knew whose wife was a little overweight was around. I think back now about how I behaved and just cringe. Around the end of that summer, an ugly mole started growing right above my right breast. I got freaked out because it was growing very fast. I went to a dermatologist and had it cut off. I thought that I had skin cancer. I stopped flaunting myself and started praying. God spoke to my spirit "that my body was His holy temple and if I didn't stop causing married men to fall into sin that He was going to allow a wasting disease to come upon me that would cause me to go bald." I was so terrified by what He said that I promised Him that I would do everything in my power to stop being a trap for others. After my ugly mole was removed, I swore that I would not do that anymore. God told me that the scar on my right breast would be a reminder to me to keep the promise I made to Him to be virtuous.

After that, I chose to do my best to be unnoticed by the opposite sex. I fell a lot of times but I got back up, asked God to please forgive me, have mercy on me, and change me. I knew I needed help to uproot this weed that was so deeply embedded in my soul.

Then Jehu went to Jezreel. When Jezebel heard about it, she painted her eyes, arranged her hair and looked out of the window.

2 Kings 9:30

For some reason when I first read this I laughed. Then, I realized just how true to our fallen nature this act of sorcery really is. Did Jezebel paint her eyes because she heard the prophecy that Jehu would kill her and she wanted to look her best on her deathbed? Or, was it simply because she just didn't feel as powerful without it?

Perhaps she just didn't want to be caught dead without her makeup?

I remember being in counseling and having the Holy Spirit tell me (in my spirit) to stop wearing makeup for a week. I was horrified and questioned if I had really heard from God. "Take ANYTHING Lord, but not my makeup, just don't go there, OK?" This was the weirdest week of my life. I remember walking around feeling so ugly and unattractive. I remember seeing an ex-boyfriend from high school in the local grocery store and feeling completely humiliated without my makeup on. I then felt God speak to my spirit, "Why are you so ashamed of the way that I created you to be? This is who you are, when you wear makeup that is the made up you." I then stopped hiding behind my hair and makeup and started to be a little bit braver, naked-faced. I realized that I was masquerading around under a plastic disguise. Some of you know exactly what I am talking about. For those of you that don't struggle with this, just bear with me for a minute. It had become a major issue in my life. I would not leave the house without my makeup on. I remember when James and I first got married if I even thought we were going to start fighting I would run over to my vanity and put my makeup on. I felt like I had better control of the fight (of him) if I had my face on. One day James and I were starting to get into it and I ran to my vanity to put my makeup on. Just then, I felt God say, "Don't forget to put your fighting face on."

    Other times, I would go to a certain function where I knew there would be men that would eyeball me. God would have the nerve to tell me to go without makeup. I know that this sounds very ridiculous, but I would actually get mad at God and accuse Him of trying to humiliate me. In fact, He was trying to protect me and rid me of this root of sorcery that was so deeply embedded in me. Other times, I would put on a certain pair of pants that made me feel incredibly sexy and He would prompt me to change. I had to stop wearing some of my favorite brands because not only did they make me feel empowered, but the company that made them stood for things that were not OK in God's eyes. My husband and I went around-and-around about my clothing. I couldn't even step out of our bedroom without him completely losing his cool over my outfit. I learned that wearing some shirts wasn't worth the fight. There were times when I wanted to dress modestly but didn't have clothing that was appropriate. Other times, I would get so fed up with my husband throwing (what I thought were fits) that I would put on the most provocative piece of clothing that I could find and walk out the door in rebellion. What I didn't understand is how this chipped away at my husband's heart. One day, I became so frustrated while dressing that God impressed upon me: "Pay attention to your husband's reaction to how you dress. If what you wear bothers him in any way, do not wear it. What's more important, the way you want to feel or the way you want your husband to feel about you?" Am I saying that you should dress in turtlenecks in the summer? No. The old saying "you are what you wear," is often totally true. Some of you are probably thinking that this is pretty drastic. The way I looked at it is God set His children apart for greatness. Who was I to argue about how He got me there? I would see my friends wearing things that God told me not to or listening to music that God told me to cut out or even drinking a cold beer when God told me not to. Honestly, saying "no" to these things made me feel deprived. I look back now and I thank God for His discipline and conviction. I would have been a completely different person without them.

You have heard that it was said, 'Do not commit adultery.' But I tell you that anyone who looks at a woman lustfully has already committed adultery with her in his heart. Jesus speaking in

Matthew 5:27

As women, we need to think differently about men looking at us. Do we want to bear the sins of causing the prophets and priests in our homes and good men to fall? Do we want to be the reason that godly men commit adultery? I cringe to think about how many men I took down in ONE day with ONE provocative shirt. I was in the world for 26 years before I gave my life to Christ. From my teenage years until I was saved and even years after, I don't even want to think of how many men I caused to fall. Ladies, I have heard and even said, "If that man looks at me in a lustful way that's his problem, not mine." We brush off all responsibility. Yet, when we stand at our closet choosing what to wear and decide to wear something that makes us feel empowered and sexy then, at that moment, it becomes our problem. This is the point where it all comes down to motives. We were born to worship. At all times we are worshiping something, whether that is our Creator or His creation. Now, I am not saying that we cannot ever dress up or feel good and confident about ourselves when we leave the house. I am not saying that we cannot wear sexy pieces for our husbands. I am saying we need to be mindful of how our attire affects those around us. We need to be balanced in this area. I don't have to go too far into this. I know you ladies understand what I'm talking about. If by our apparel, we are causing the men around us to look upon us in an unclean way, then we are partly responsible for any sin of impurity that might occur. And yes, there will be that occasional male who will undress you with his eyes, regardless of what you are wearing. That's not what I'm talking about here. We need to become so secure in who we are on the inside that we do not have to draw attention to our outward appearance. Some women (including me, at one time) are walking around like advertisements. LADIES, WE ARE NOT FOR SALE!!!

I truly believe that pornography is a double-sided coin. Men would not be tempted to look at us, if we were not willing to pose half naked for them. We need to rise above this lie.

We need to be accountable for our choices. We need to teach our daughters these important lessons.

We cheapen ourselves when we dress in a provocative way. Let's stop giving ourselves away for free! WE ARE PRICELESS! Let us remember that how we dress affects those around us whether we want it to or not, it does. Ask yourself who you truly want to represent. When you stand before your closet every morning trying to choose what to wear, remember you are a woman of noble character.

Women are to be respected and honored and that starts with respecting ourselves! We are the face of Christ in female form to this world. Let us be strong and bold and proud to be women of God. Let our husband's walk alongside us, knowing that they can trust us with their hearts. Let us remember that we do not need to act or dress like the women of this world to be beautiful. We do not need to control or manipulate the men around us to be affirmed as valuable. Each of us has the mind of Christ, which allows us to be tender, pure, loving, and sacred. We are to be cherished and deemed precious. We should refuse to be conformed to the image of this world. We will rise up and be a generation of virtuous women of God. We are the PURE bride of Christ. Let us act and dress like we mean it!

PART 2

REDEEMING THE JEWELS WITHIN

When I lived in Florida, I ran into one of the girls that I had previously worked with at a restaurant. While we were in the checkout line at one of the grocery stores in St. Petersburg she pulled out a huge wad of cash to pay her bill. I was curious to know what she had been up to since the last time we had worked together at the restaurant. She told me that she was pole dancing and that I should try it. I was incredibly surprised. Being from Montana I knew nothing about pole dancing. I seriously thought it was something that the movie industry made up to sell those low budget pornographic movies. It was off season at Blue Birds restaurant and few tourists were frequenting Johns Pass considering that it was hurricane season. I wasn't pulling in a 10th of the tips that I had during the busy season. Considering I was only making $2.13 an hour as a tipped employee she convinced me that I could make three times the tips that I was making at the restaurant even as a cocktail waitress at the club.

I thought long and hard about it on my drive home that night. Thoughts of dancing and actually making more money were going through my head as I passed by the night lights of 49th street. The evening air was hot and smelled of some kind of industrial smoke and sulfur as I pondered, "Could I seriously break every moral that I was ever taught in my wholesome upbringing? Could I really allow a bunch of perverts to look at my body in order to make my rent and buy supplies for baby and me?" I remember spending the last of my money on diapers, gas and a flamethrower from Wendy's. As I picked up the baby from the sitters I went home to my shotgun apartment were the tap water was almost as hot as the Florida winter air. After feeding, bathing and rocking the baby to sleep I took a long look at my situation and knew I had to do something different. My fridge was completely empty, I was out of toilet paper and other supplies, the landlord was leaving eviction notices on my front door handle (which was held shut by a metal clothes hanger) and I was out of cash. "Why wasn't my husband here to help me pay these bills and take care of our baby?" As I opened the front door the hot, night air hit me and I longed for the coolness of the freshwater lakes back in Montana. My coral flowered sundress swayed in the breeze and reminded me of how far away from home I truly was. I sat down on my front doorstep burrowing my bare feet in the seashell walkway that headed down to the bay. I could almost see the ocean sprays from my little, two bedroom apartment. I was one street over from the inlet. I truly did love Florida. The seagulls cried out as I realized the many questions going through my pounding head "What's going to happen to us?" "Am I going to be able to feed this baby next week?" "And diaper her and make sure she has a place to live?" "How are we going to survive?" As my toes slipped further under the warm crushed seashells the sensation brought me fully alive and somehow at that moment a mad need to survive aroused in me and I knew I had to make a choice. I couldn't go back home defeated. As my head came off the door frame and my back straightened I wiped away the exhaustion tears and something within me grew warmer and a decision had been made in my subconscious almost without my knowledge. The realization of the choice came forth and I spoke it out loud without even knowing that it had bypassed my moral compass. "It doesn't matter if it kills me I will do whatever it takes to take care of my baby!"

The next day after kissing my sweet, three-month-old daughter goodbye and handing her off to my mother in law I called in sick to the restaurant and took a detour to "THE NAMELESS GIRLS CLUB," as I pulled up into the almost empty parking lot the pink neon sign flashing, "GIRLS! GIRLS! GIRLS!" almost made me turn on my stilettos and run. The whole scene reminded me of just how far away from my Rocky Mountain upbringing that I was. There was an overpass bridge just to the south of the building and random heaps of weeds growing up the wall, sporadically. The air was hot and muggy with no breeze causing my long, blonde hair to stick to the sweat on the back of my neck. While straitening my black, thigh-high skirt I was hoping I looked halfway presentable. I noticed a few people under the overpass beyond the club and wondered if they lived under there? I remember going into the place thinking "Ok, in a few days I'll make some money for my rent, diapers, and maybe a little food and gas and then I'll be out of here." With the opening of the door came a gust of smoke, cheap perfume, whiskey and some kind of deep fried food. That actually made my empty stomach growl. A group of people were huddling over by the stage and turned and looked at me like a hungry pack of wolves. I was seriously contemplating running until my stomach growled again. "What the heck am I doing here?" This older lady came up to me and asked me if I was the new dancer. I told her I was not a dancer, but rather looking for a cocktail position. She convinced me that I was dancing material and could make much more on the dance floor. So, I asked her what she wanted me to do.

Looking around the dark, smoke-filled club I did not see my friend anywhere. My eyes couldn't get past the pole that a blonde haired girl was dancing at. The way she moved was so intimidating. The older lady told me she was giving dancing lessons and asked me to join in. I timidly agreed and felt like I was the only one she was giving lessons to. She told me that she would take care of me and get me anything that I needed. That got my full attention. Until another dancer in deep purple lingerie took the stage. "At what cost?" My inner self-questioned. The older lady took me to a back room, gave me a show name, took a Polaroid picture of me, and introduced me to a man and other dancers in the dressing room. She gave me my own mirror and stool. Some of the girls looked very threatened by me. Next to me was a dancer in her late 40's that had dedicated her life to the profession. She had four children and didn't expect to stop pole dancing any time soon. I remember the other dancers talking about a man that took care of them and didn't allow this or that. I don't remember his name, but I do remember that he was the one I was introduced to in the back room. They posted my picture on the "Wall of Fame" with all the other dancers. They did that to have a record of girls in case any of them turned up missing. My eyes looked over the poster board and did not see my friend's picture anywhere. When I was sitting on the stool putting on my makeup and glitter, I felt very unnerved and realized one of the other younger dancers was watching me. "That used to be Kasey's spot" she announced with a very sad, hostile look. "I didn't know. I can move if you have another mirror," I assured her trying to keep the peace. She pointed at the obituary on the wall that pictured a beautiful young woman with waist-length platinum blonde hair. She was so pretty. The flyer said she was found dead. "What happened, if I might ask?" "Kasey was the best dancer in this place. She could out dance all of us. She could drink us all under the table when it came to vodka." By this time, most of the girls were listening and looking at her picture. "Kasey overdosed a while back. God, may there be vodka in heaven." As they all acknowledged the picture and agreed, I felt chills run up and down my spine and wondered for the thousandth time what the heck I was doing there. Thoughts of my sweet daughter kept running through my mind as my breasts ached to hold her close. "Yes, I must remain focused on keeping my apartment and taking care of my daughter." At that split second, I remembered thinking that I should become a writer so I could write about all these beautiful women who felt like this was the only life that they could possibly lead. It felt like a completely different world in that dressing room. With all the pink glitter, feathers and costumes it was almost like all the little princesses had grown up and stopped believing in fairy tales. Their reality was broken dreams, broken hearts, and broken lives.

"Showtime!" my heart skipped a few beats as the smell of vodka, sweat, cigarette smoke, and cheap perfumed filled the air. The lady three times my age reassured me that I was going to be great because I was born to dance. I confided in the older dancer that I was scared and didn't want to do it anymore. She reassured me that she and three of the other girls would go out there with me and that I had nothing to fear. The music started and we all went out on the stage. The stage was big and shaped in a half circle. It reminded me of an old theater stage in an opera house. There weren't a whole lot of men there yet, considering that it was still early in the evening. The music was of a slow techno beat that was a little bit hard to move to but as soon as I felt I had my rhythm I turned around and realized that I was the only one left on the dance floor. I tried to run off the stage, but the girls blocked the door and kept yelling at me to dance. The other men started to notice the new dancer and came closer to the stage whistling and telling me to keep dancing. Timidly I took the stage alone. My mind wandered back home to the streams of fresh water, cool, crisp mountain air and the fields of daisies. The smoke was thick and most of the men had already had plenty to drink. Because it was a "modest" club, I was able to keep my undergarments on. The music stopped and men from around the club approached the stage and started throwing dollar bills and yelling for an encore. I looked back at the other girls who were standing in the doorway smiling at me and telling me to pick up my money. So, I gathered up all the dollar bills, turned and pushed my way past the girls and into the dressing room. "I have to get out of here. I can't breathe. What am I doing? Did I want to end up like some of these ladies who had children at home waiting for them while they wasted their lives entertaining drunken men? What about the girl in the picture whose eyes were so haunting? Did I want to end up dead like her?" I started shaking as I frantically gathered my things. My mind raced as I rushed out the back door. Night had fallen and I quickly ran to my car unlocked it, jumped in and locked the door. "What are you doing, Angela?" I scolded myself. I could feel the warm tears flowing down my cheeks as I fumbled to turn over the ignition. I caught a glimpse of myself in the rear view mirror and realized how far away from my childhood self I had become. The tears wouldn't stop coming as I raced a crossed the bay bridge trying to get my car to take flight. Somehow the city lights haunted me that night as I wondered how much longer I'd be able to avoid my landlord before baby and I were living underneath that overpass I just speed away from. For the first time, I really wanted to move home. I went to the sitters snagged up my sweet Autumn and took her home to snuggle her all night. I laid in bed with her curled under my breast fast asleep, as I laid awake most of the night wondering about our future together. I knew we at least had that night that we could be safely tucked into bed without anyone knocking on our door trying to kick us out. Morning came too quickly. I was desperate enough to dance there one more night. That night I actually had a man follow me to my car. All the dancers were instructed to leave the building in twos but it seemed like every night I was trying to escape from the life I had created and would frantically run out the back door. I went to a different club to try and get away from him, but he followed me there, also. A week later, it was reported that a dancer in a club across town had been found dead in the outside dumpster. I was done. No amount of tips was worth my life. A few weeks later I had a stalker come to my house. Trying to get inside he turned off the breaker to my power, knocked my vogue magazine out of the bathroom window, and tried to crawl through the window. I don't know if it was the same guy from the club or the homeless man who lived in the alley behind my apartment. Not only did I stop dancing but I also had to move out of South Pasadena and in with a friend in Tampa. I spent many sleepless nights trying to quite my screaming baby for fear that I wouldn't be able to hear the intruder. When I was dancing in the club, I could feel the dancer's deep pains and sorrows that they tried to drown by using various substances. The hopelessness of ever becoming something different filled every inch of the dressing room. Don't get me wrong some of the younger women enjoyed what they did to a degree but some felt trapped in their lifestyle. I left so grieved for these women even though I hardly knew them. Something in me wanted them to have so much more. I wanted to save them all but at that point in time, I had no clue how to help them.

I want to say to any stripper/pole dancer who is reading this book that there is another way. You can find redemption at the end of the rainbow. You can be freed from the life you are leading. You can become a woman that your children are proud of. I need to tell you something. Even though I only danced a few times, it was very hard for me to share this part of my life with anyone, especially my husband and children. While writing this chapter, I felt that I had to share this part of my life with my husband and older teenage daughters. For the longest time, I was so scared they would look down on me because of my past choices. They did not. Instead, my girls laughed hysterically. God had changed me and healed me so much that my daughters couldn't even see me as a pole dancer. It was amusing to them to even think of me in such a way. They joked about it and called me by my show name. My oldest daughter said, "Mom if God can change you, He can change anyone." She told me that the story of my dancing experience did not embarrass her. Rather, it helped her to understand that no matter what we become by our own poor choices; God can always redeem us from it. I was so proud of my daughters and honored that they could see the transformation in me.

You will be called by a new name that the mouth of the Lord will bestow. You will be a royal diadem in the hand of your God.

Isaiah 62: ½ of 2 & 3.

I had no clue that I was fearfully and wonderfully made. I had no idea that God set me apart for a greater purpose than what I saw on a daily basis, growing up. I dreamt of more but didn't know that I was **created** for more.

Before I formed you in the womb I knew (chose) you before you were born I set you apart; I appointed you as a prophet to the nations."

Jeremiah 1:5

I think that we all get a little muddy growing up. I think that there are always things in our past that we wished we could change. But, time and circumstances are what makes us who we are today. We all have a little bit of shattered glass in our past; it's all about what we do with those broken pieces that matter.

The Lord is close to the brokenhearted and saves those who are crushed in spirit.

Psalms 34:18

Can God truly find the jewel in this Nile? When we feel like all is lost and we are too tarnished to be washed and purified, think again for your Maker has sent me here to inform you that if He can purify me, He can purify you.

You turned my wailing into dancing; You removed my sackcloth and clothed me with joy, that my heart may sing to you and not be silent. O Lord my God, I will give you thanks forever.

Psalms 30:11 & 12

So, hold your head high for He will not deny you. He has sent me to alert you that He can allure you; He can lead you into the desert and speak tenderly to you. He will give you back your vineyards, and make the Valley of Achor a door of hope for you. It is there that you will sing as in the days of your youth. (Derived from Hosea 2:14 &15.)

Therefore I am now going to allure her; I will lead her into the desert and speak tenderly to her. There I will give her back her vineyards and will make the Valley of Achor a door of hope. There she will sing as in the days of her youth, as in the day she came up out of Egypt.

Hosea 2:14&15

Restoration is yours for the taking.

5 TELL ME SWEET LITTLE LIES (VENUS)

We have a feminine heart. We were made to be soft, gentle, and admired. When the feminine heart gets broken by the opposite sex, it retreats. The heart will seek a place to hide, be accepted, and rest. If this means to rest in the arms of another hurting heart, then that's where it will find its "rest".

We think that we are doing ourselves a favor by retreating into someone who understands our pain and longs to heal our wounds. Let me ask you a question and I really want you to think deeply about this question. If you have hidden in other hearts for years, let me boldly ask how long did they give you that comfort? Think back on the other hearts that you have gone to, seeking healing, peace, and comfort how long was it, a year, a week; perhaps, a night? How long was it before you could see that their heart was just as damaged as yours and they could offer no healing balm for your own heart?

It didn't take long for me to figure out that another human being could not heal what was so devastatingly broken within me. So, I searched for someone or something to heal my brokenness that I could not even touch or know the depths of. The woman's heart is like an ancient scroll, it records all from the day you were born until the day you breathe your last. Wow! How on earth could anyone, ANYONE possibly, fully, decipher a woman's heart? No, it's not humanly possible. It's just not. No matter how that other person makes you feel for a short period of time, after a while both of your hurting hearts will start to surface and demand from the other one, healing. It just doesn't work. Healing, full, wholehearted healing can only come from the one who created the heart. No, I'm not talking about Venus.

For I will restore health to you and your wounds I will heal, declares the Lord.

~Jeremiah 30:17

Song of Solomon states "Do not awaken love before it so desires." In my case, it was awakened before I even knew desire. I played a lot of "doctor" when I was young; sometimes with boys, other times with girls. This was a game of inspecting each other's parts (or that's how we were taught to play, anyway). I can't remember ever not being called sexy, even when I was very little. I was very confused about my sexuality. I was very drawn to a lot of different people growing up.

I was married, had two children, and going through my first divorce before I even entertained the thought of acting out on my same-sex tendencies. At that time in my life, I was so severely hurt by men that I chalked them all up to being pigs. All men were pigs, in my eyes. I had such a severe hatred towards the way men had treated me. This deep seeded wound led me to choose to have a same-sex relationship with another woman.

I understand that these subjects are not the most popular subjects to talk about, but there is no reason to pretend that they don't happen. These are the monsters in the closet that need to come out. There is a reason that I have been lead to share these things. Some of you have been through similar situations and need to be healed as I was.

I've heard it to be said that "Through every battle, a song is born." Allow me to share this part of my life with you so that you too perhaps may learn to sing again...

MY DARKEST DAYS

After my first husband left me for the second time, my mother and older sister thought it would be best for me to move back to our hometown and work at the local sawmill. So, my daughters (4 years and 6 months old) and I moved home and I got a job at the local sawmill. A few of the men in our family had worked there including my stepdad and brother-in-law. Very few women worked there; only the ones who could cut it. I had two children to support and take care of so, off I went to the most strenuous job that I ever had. I started in the pit on the roundtable. The roundtable was this huge 20 foot round metal table that would turn as boards would get cut to length and fall on it. This was the last process of the mill and the planer. Our job as "the pit crew" was to pull the boards off by length and stack them on the right bundle.

After doing that for 8 to 12 hours, I just knew I was either going to make it or die, but I was not going to quit. I remember coming home black and blue with splinters a half inch long in my arms and legs

A few months into the job one of the pit crew lowered a bundle of 200 some odd boards on to the top of my foot, permanently crushing the tiny bones in the top of it. This particular worker was so cute that I later married him. I took a few days off to recover from my injury and then went back to work. Nothing was going to stop me. Some workers in the mill and planer were taking bets on how long I would last. I don't think any of them won their bets. I probably would have made fun of me too if I was introduced to my 5'4 platinum blonde self. I was tan and wore my "sex wax surfing" t-shirt from Florida. I was not fit to be doing this kind of job. But, something inside of me wouldn't quit. I had two babies at home counting on me and I craved the recognition that would come with defeating the job. Two years later, I through in the towel. I was tired, worn out, bruised, beaten, harassed and had my fill. I wore my wedding ring from my first marriage for the longest time. I'm not sure if it even mattered. I think I got hit on more while wearing it, mostly by other married men.

At the time, I felt that men had taken everything from me and had given me nothing in return. I also knew that there was not one man on earth I could count on. I was so discouraged that I wanted nothing to do with men.

ALL MEN WERE PIGS! (That was my motto for men). I was tired of being just a piece of meat.

While in this environment a few of the women hit on me and wanted to experiment. It all started out as fun and games. Just a few drinks after work, a little dirty dancing, with the right music, and a little teasing in the dark bar, "No harm done," right? I had no clue the door that I had opened at the time. After a few times of experimenting with a few of the girls, one of the women who professed to be gay and I kept experimenting, drinking and hanging out more and more. I never thought I would take it as far as I did. It went from experimentation to relations before I even knew it. I felt I would never be with another man for as long as I lived.

I drank a lot of booze, trying to extinguish the reality of not being "normal". If to be normal meant being deeply hurt by men, submitting to them, and then staying that way for the rest of my life, then I wanted nothing to do with being "normal." That was my mindset. The pit crew and I would go drinking almost every night after work. I still remember the looks on my mother's face when I would come home drunk at 3:00 or 4:00 o' clock in the morning. One night while she had been watching my children, I came in, made up some excuse, headed straight for the toilet, and fell off trying to go pee. I remember watching her leave in silence. The next morning she was very disappointed with me. I was disappointed with myself, but I didn't know how to get out of the hole I had dug. Coming home drunk became a normal ritual for me. I drank very heavily back then. My children were very angry with me for not being home with them. My oldest started kindergarten and attended school from 8 AM to 3:30 PM. I started the night shift at 2:30 PM and didn't get off work until 11:00PM. Every month, our crew would switch from day shift to night shift or vice versa. While on the night shift, I hardly ever got to see my oldest daughter. I remember her having my Mom help her write little letters in which she would tell me how much she missed me and how much she wished that she had a mommy who could stay home and a daddy who would do her mommy's job. Then, her mommy could stay home and play with her all day. One time, I came home from work and squatted down on the kitchen floor to say "hi" to my youngest daughter, who was around one and a half years old. She was so mad at me for not being home with her that she grabbed a hold of my hair and pulled me down. I fell off balance and bounced my head off the kitchen floor.

My darkest days occurred when I would try to hide my same-sex relationship from my children and family.

My mother already knew. I would lie, hide things, drink more, and not come home right after work. Deep down I knew what I was doing was not right. But I had convinced myself that I didn't have the strength to care. I would swear to myself that I would never allow another man to strip me of who I was again. I didn't care whether the mill workers knew what I was doing or not. I bragged about it in the break room in order to draw people away from my hurting heart. I felt so ashamed, but never let on that I wasn't in control. In no way shape or form would I become the victim of men. I would ask myself, if this is so right, why does it feel so wrong? I was too over-worked and too tired to care.

THE CALLING

The spring of 2001, the planer got shut down for a week. I remember getting some kind of tax return, which I used to travel to the ocean, sit on the beach and smell the salty air. I didn't care how far I had to travel. I just wanted to sit on the beach and drink a strawberry margarita. So, off we (my female friend and I) went, packing our kids in the car and dragging them across the states to the ocean. We stayed in a seaside shack with a big sliding glass door overlooking the ocean. Everyone had fallen fast asleep that night. The shades were open and, as I stoked the woodstove, I kept feeling like there was someone out there watching me. I didn't feel afraid or scared. Rather, I felt ashamed, dirty, and unnerved. What was this about? I never felt this way before. I fell into a daze and as the stormy night lights flashed, I saw a man standing on the beach outside of the sliding glass doors looking in, with sad, longing eyes. I wanted to give him what he wanted. What did he want? I felt such a longing for whoever this was. I could feel his love and yearning to rescue me and take me far away from there. I knew he had come for me. I remember staring out at the stormy sea for what seemed like hours. I knew whoever that man was, I had to be with him and he longed to be with me.

After that night, I knew my life would never be the same. I didn't realize until years later that the man I saw at the beach was Christ; watching, yearning, desiring to love and protect me, and rescue me from the bondage of the life I had chosen. The Creator of the Universe wanted to be a part of my life.

Did I immediately go home and give my life to this man? No. But, I knew in that ocean hut that if I didn't give up the reins, I was going to destroy myself and possibly my children, too.

When I got home from the beach, I knew something had to change. I knew that the life I was leading and the choices I was making were leading me to death. My oldest daughter, who was now six, wanted to start praying for a new daddy and a husband for me. I went along with her, feeling like I was probably a big joke in heaven and God probably didn't want to hear my prayers. I felt that I was a big disappointment to Him and to my family, But, I prayed anyway because I knew that it was important to my daughter. And then, God heard my sweet, little daughter's prayers and answered them. A few weeks later I met James. When James came into my life, he kept saying, "I wish I would have met you when you were younger." I knew he could feel my brokenness. I tried to break up with him, to get him away from my bleeding heart but, God had other plans. I knew I had nothing left to offer. His family would often remind me of how lucky I was to have such a good man that loved and accepted me. I knew this was true and it somehow made me feel all the more worthless. I felt second-rate, second hand, and like a little used up rag doll. I knew I had nothing to offer him. Nevertheless, he persisted and asked me to marry him. I knew that God had softened my heart because I decided to try one more time. If this one broke what was left of my heart, I was completely done. My children were very happy, and I started to believe that just maybe I could learn to love again. So, I said, "Yes."

      Ladies, let me tell you how deeply my past had hurt my new husband. Even though James knew that I had a sexual history, I don't think he really understood the depths of it until we became soul tied. James and I were intimate on our second night together (initiated by me). There was absolutely no foundation of trust laid in our marriage. I had no boundaries when it came to sex. I was so afraid that James would find out my darkest secrets, learn that I was truly not worth anything, and leave me. I actually expected it to happen over and over throughout our marriage. I was not his virgin bride. I was not the one he fell in love with at first glance. He did not vow to work seven years for my love like Jacob did. (Genesis 29) No, I gave him all that I had left the second night we were together. My second husband had a very empty marriage. At the time, I felt there was nothing I could do about it. I kept reminding him that he knew what he was getting into when we married.

James and I were already married and in the processes of having our second child together when I opened my little, black book. That was not the time to be telling dark secrets. These things grieved my husband deeply and he regretted marrying me and allowing me to be the mother of his children. I felt sad for the way that I had deeply grieved him, but there was nothing I could do about my past. I couldn't change it. We were engaged for a year and right after we got married I got saved. I was a Christian and Christ was working on healing me through that time, but I had gone so deep and so far into the world that the healing process took years for me.

RUN TO THE BATTLE

When I was in the same-sex relationship, I felt abandoned by all. I just needed someone to get down on my level, see me in all of my sins and just love me, offer me a handout and let me know that I was worth saving. Not once did anyone come to me in love and offer prayer or a way out of the situation that I was in. All I felt was condemnation and accusations. At the depth that I was in, there was no way I was getting out of that Labyrinth by myself. I needed help.

I know that there will be people who think less of me after they read this book. But, I also know this book is not for those people, it is for the lost and hopeless people who feel like they have gone too far off the deep end for Christ to save and restore them. I have already settled it in my heart. If my story only helps one person, it was worth writing. As Christians, we also need to remember the pit that we were in before Christ reached down and rescued us.

The condemnation was strong and the accusations kept coming. "You're going to burn in hell for this one," accused one good-intentioned Christian. We (Christians) think that this kind of behavior is going to make them (sinners) wake up and want to give their lives to Christ but it actually has the reverse effect. This kind of attitude actually sabotages our prayers for them, agrees with the enemies plans for their lives, and turns them away from the right path. I know and understand that sometimes we seriously have no clue how to deal with these kinds of situations. Let's try to hate the sin, love the sinner. For we all fall short of the glory of God and we are all sinners in some way or another. Condemnation does not come from God or help those that are lost in this confusing battle. Let us love those who profess to be gay and understand that Jesus bled and died for all mankind. They are worth saving too!

I need to make one thing clear here; I know now that sex is a beautiful thing when engaged within biblical boundaries, one man, one woman, one marriage bed. Sex was created by God to reproduce and for the pleasure of enhancing our marriage experience. Sex outside of these safe boundaries produces scars, teen pregnancies, unplanned pregnancies, fatherlessness, sexually transmitted diseases, heartbreak, unhealthy soul ties, lust, perversion, violent acts of passion, rage, possessiveness, etc.

I belong to my lover, and his desire is for me. Come, my lover, let us go to the countryside, let us spend the night in the villages. Let us go early to the vineyards to see if the vines have budded if their blossoms have opened, and if the pomegranates are in bloom- there I will give you my love.

Song of Songs 7:10-12

There is nothing more sacred and satisfying than making love to the one who truly loves and respects you and is completely committed to the marriage. It's a deep sense of belonging and a security that you cannot find anywhere else on earth. It's a place of freedom. It's a place of beauty.

One day I had a non-believer call me on my cell phone crying because a believer had hurt her. She cried, "Why would I ever want to become a Christian? So I could go around telling my non-believing friends that they are bound for hell?" Still crying she proclaimed, "No WAY! No thank you, that kind of Christianity is not for me." This woman was so incredibly hurt by a believer who was condemning her that she wanted nothing to do with Christianity. My heart went out to her knowing how she felt. When I prayed for her later on, I felt lead to tell her that, "You are precious in God's site, He wants you to know that you are not forgotten and He hears your prayers." I truly believe that this is what He wanted me to relay to her. I believe the same message is true for all of you who feel forgotten by God because of this state you were lead to believe that you were born into. This mindset you feel that you will never break out of and for those of you who have been so severely condemned by your friends and family that you have contemplated taking your life. Let me say it again, you are precious, you are not forgotten and your prayers are being heard. Jesus knew that you were worth fighting and dying for.

Jesus tells us to go into the entire world and preach the gospel. If we read Mathew, Mark, Luke, and John, we see the perfect example of how Jesus loved the sinners and tried to turn them from their ways through His love. His greatest commandment:

Jesus replied: "'Love the Lord your God with all your heart and with all your soul and with all your mind.' This is the first and greatest commandment. And second is like it: 'Love your neighbor as yourself.' All the Law and the Prophets hang on these two commandments."

Matthew 22: 37-40

I do not believe that God would create only a select few in His image and others in a perverse image that was destined to be scorned and confused for their lives on Earth. God does not want anyone to perish.

> *For God so loved the WORLD, He gave His only begotten son that WHOSOEVER believeth in Him should not perish but have everlasting life.*
>
> *John 3:16 (emphasis added).*

Some of us have heard this verse so many times, but I implore you to stop and think about it for a second. God said "WHOSOEVER." Come one, come all, only believeth in Him. This invitation extends to all who choose to believe. This dear friend is the key.

What exactly does that mean? Why do you think you are who you are, because you were created that way or because time and circumstances happen to us all? Because you were born to lust after women or because the environment you grew up in promoted demeaning women? Or perhaps you were sexually abused at an early age and left to believe that you were born to please those who desired that of you? Or maybe you were lead to believe that you were not worthy of love but only good for one thing? Or maybe you were like me and felt like the opposite sex thought all you were was someone to cook, clean, and decorate their home with your appearance. However, you have been lead to believe that you are the way you are I am here to tell you that I know the One who created you and he is ready to heal your inner wounds.

There is one man who walked the face of this Earth and not once pinned a woman up as a calendar girl; not once demeaned her in any way. He looked upon her with kindness and compassion as the weaker sex, never to hurt, never to control, never to order or expect anything in return for his offerings. Gentleness was his nature and still is. Women are fully alive in his presence and he longs to hear, listen, and understand the fullness of a woman's heart and the depths of a woman's soul. He wants to heal the brokenness of a woman's spirit.

Let me take a few minutes and speak to those who have been sexually abused, "Sweet, Precious Child, no matter what happened in your past you are still as precious today as the day you came forth from your mother's womb. God never intended for you to be so severely hurt. You were never created to be used by man. You were created to live a life of exuberant peace, to love and be loved in the purest form. The plans that God had for you then, He has for you now. The same child you were before the abuse is the same child you are now. It was not your fault and it has not altered the purpose for which you were created. Yes, it has altered many things but not the purpose for your life. You are more than the aftermath of other people's horrific choices. You are not a mistake you were planned before the creation of the world. Your Creator planned what color your hair would be, what color your eyes would be, what color your skin would be what your voice would sound like and the purpose for which you were formed. But no He did not plan for your abuser to abuse you. Sin came into the world with the fall of Adam. And it grieved God and He wept and flooded the earth because of it (see Genesis 6).

Regardless of what has happened you are loved and sought after.

I feel the need right now to stand in for anyone who has ever hurt you, abused you or caused you to feel like less of a human being. I want you to think of that person right now. Your uncle, teacher, babysitter, acquaintance, etc. and I want to stand in the gap for them and ask you to "Please forgive me? Please forgive my ignorance and harsh words towards you. Please forgive me for treating you like less than a human. Please forgive me for rejecting you, shunning you and hurting you. I am so sorry. I was wrong. Please forgive me?"

Father God, I come before You now on behalf of these beautiful women that You love. I know that You see their pain and all that they have had to endure. Some of their lives have been unimaginable, too much for them to bear. They have been abused, forsaken, shunned and forgotten by those who once loved them. Their hearts have been torn and shattered. But You see and You know their scars. These women are so precious to You. I ask God that You intervene. Hear my cry for Your beautiful women and meet them right where they are tonight and be their Love, be their Healer, be their Redeemer. I ask for redemption and restitution for these precious jewels. Please comfort them now like You would a precious child. Thank you, Father, that You hear my prayers and answer them.

Angelina B. B.

6

Redemption

To: My Hero, My Rescuer…..I am eternally grateful.

The day that changed my life forever was October 10th 2002. It was a crisp, fall day and we had a guest speaker come to our church. I knew that I needed to give my life back to Christ knowing that He was my only hope of ever changing. I knew that my life was in desperate need of being saved and that I had made a complete mess out of it.

That evening, I listened to our guest speaker preach his message. When he gave the altar call, my heart started beating so fast I knew I was either going to give my life to Christ or die. I knew that I was not going to leave that church the same way I went in.

I waited for the church to clear out before I started walking down that aisle, feeling like I was entering another realm. I could almost see myself going from darkness into the light. I felt the presence of Christ and His angels waiting for me at the altar. When I reached the altar, I started crying so hard and for so long. It was like a whole lifetime of pain and sorrow just lifted off of me. When I finally got up, I felt so light and free. My heart soared and I knew that I had given my life to Jesus. I've never taken it back. This is one choice that I have never regretted. I see now that with that one choice not only did I save myself from the fires of hell, but I changed the life course of my children and their children as well. I had changed history and my children's lineage. We were now adopted into the family of Christ.

I want to give you an entry I made in my journal that night just so you can understand a little better how that day affected me.

October 10th 2002

Tonight is the beginning of my eternal life. My name means more tonight than comprehended by the human mind. My tears fall, my heart soars. Peace, nothing but love that I have never felt before. I am a piece of something unknowingly powerful. I know there is a place for little, bitty me in the mists of angels and apostles.

I will reign with the holiest of holy people and God Almighty, Himself. Caress me with your everlasting breath. Breathe into me the song of thanksgiving and send your angels to watch over me and kiss me sweetly on my eyelids. Rejoice for today is the day that will forever change my life. Help me, Father, to never stray, never turn my back.

When I fall, help me to grow closer to you through that stumbling block. Tonight, I am overwhelmed with Your presence and intimacy. Help me to love others the way You love me. Sing through my voice and touch nations. Help me to humble myself like my children and fall on my face in front of my God, You! God of Abraham, You complete me. Please Lord; help me be strong in You.

Rejoice, for today is my birthday because I have been born again!

I want you to know and understand it is just that easy. You too are one choice away from your eternal destiny. Before I met Christ, I really didn't understand how easy it was to be saved. I was one choice away from choosing the life that Christ died to give me. Redemption is a beautiful thing. A chaotic life placed in the hands of God can turn into a life worth living. Trust me on this one. Away from God, I had no real purpose. I had dreams and talents, but placed in the hands of God I became His masterpiece. When we live our own life apart from God, we try to create what we think we should do and have. But, when we give our lives, talents, and dreams back to the One who created them in us, our purpose has nowhere else to go besides back out through us. We can choose between life and death, blessings and curses. (see Deuteronomy 30:15&16) All we have to do is choose. Are we going to continue down the road we are on with hopes of finding a better tomorrow, or are we going to give our life back to God knowing He holds the keys to our purpose for tomorrow? It's our choice. What will you choose today? Today could be the day that your name means more than it ever could or has in the past. Your name could be written right next to mine (in gold) in the Lamb's book of life!

Choose you this day whom you will serve, yourself or the One who wrote the blueprints for your life?

I guarantee that if you choose to lay it all down and follow God, your life will not be easy, but it will be worth living.

Being a believer is not for the faint of heart. Believers need to be brave, strong, mighty warriors for Christ. We are to storm the gates of hell and release those from darkness (see Isaiah 61:1). We must face many trials in this life and prevail. The difference for the believers is that when we live our lives on purpose, we do not live it alone. I have never felt alone as a follower. When all the others left me, even my best friend, God never left me. He picked me up and carried me. He guides, directs, loves, leads, and protects me. He provides for me and is my all in all. There will be times in your walk with God that He will ask you to hold on to the ship as you go through the high seas. He may not rescue you in the storm, but He will always be there strengthening you to preserve in it. He will imprint upon your heart that you can trust Him and that He's got your back during the most intense heartaches.

One day during the last year, I was in church getting prayer when I saw myself as a black sparrow with two arrows piercing my heart. My heart has been severely pierced twice by betrayal. At that moment, I experienced God's tenderness toward me. When I got home, I looked up the meaning of a sparrow. This is what I found.

In the early days of pirates, one of the reasons a sailor would get a sparrow tattoo was to symbolize his perseverance in crossing a high sea.

The sparrow also means loyalty, rebirth, and freedom.

After I looked up the meaning of a sparrow, I realized that my vision meant that I had flown across a very high sea. Even though I was pierced during that flight, I made it across the sea safely because of the strength and courage God had given me. During this very painful time in my life, my God never left me, but neither did He rescue me. He allowed me to face those hurricane size waves with Him so that I would know and understand that He is with me. He was loyal through it and on the other side of off that heartache I found rebirth and freedom.

My point in all this is that becoming a Christian is very easy; staying a Christian is the challenge. But, if, through your journey on this Earth, you choose God, you will never walk down any road alone. I guarantee that in the end, it will all have been worth it to have put your trust in Him. For every tear shed, every battle wound, every sacrifice will be rewarded in the end.

TEARS IN A BOTTLE

The other day I was listening to a teaching on "your emotions." In this teaching, the speaker said something about how God has every tear in a bottle. Right then and there, I stopped the CD. "God has every tear in a bottle?" I thought to myself. "You mean to tell me that God has been with me throughout my whole life, not just the years that I chose to walk with Him but every second of every day of every year of my thirty-three years?" These thoughts overwhelmed me to the point of having screaming tears streaking down both checks. God has all of my tears, tears of failure, tears of remorse, and tears of guilt? He holds my tears from when I didn't graduate from high school because I cheated on my extra credit, tears from when my first husband left me and went to prison? Tears from when I lost my job, my rent and electricity bill were due, I had hardly any food in my shotgun apartment, a baby on its way, and I was 3,000 miles away from home? Every tear that has fallen He has?

He has the tears from when my first husband left me for the second time and my second child was born and I had to go back to work and leave her at a week old, in daycare? He was there. For every second of every day of every moment of my life, He was there? I thought: I have had a pretty dramatic life and God has a lot of people to talk to. Does He actually have time to sit down with little old me and go through every hurt every sorrow, every single tear in my life, and tell me what He was thinking at that time? How he was feeling at that time. And then it dawned on me that we will have eternity together. Of course, He will have time for me. He has all the time that He desires to spend with me. I could just see us in heaven. I get there and Jesus walks over to me with his sandaled feet and robe, and a bottle of tears in hand. He sits down and starts going through the stories and I look up and see all the millions of souls standing in line waiting to talk to Jesus. I say "Is now really a good time?" "I mean, You have all these other people who need your attention, do you really want to take a lifetime with me?" He gently touches my arm and love flows through me and He speaks: "Of course I do. You mean the world to me. Your love for me shows in how many people know you here and my love for you shows in you being here. Be still and know that I am God. When you walked through the water I was there and through the flames, you were not burned. You did not drown because I was with you. Now let's discuss these tears."

 Filled with love and not able to take my eyes off my King, I sit and listen for a lifetime or more; however long it takes for Him to explain how much he was a part of my life, all the turns I missed, and all the souls I helped to save. The choices I caused other people to make when they asked for help and I turned my back. He would show me all the unopened gifts and all the times that he protected my children because I had asked Him too. The day that I was meant to die before I knew Him and the day I ended up being on His path. The God who created the stars loves you and me so much that He cares about every detail, aspect, and every single tear that falls.

 When I was thirty years old, God spoke to my spirit. I had pulled into the grocery store to get some food for dinner. It was muggy and hot. I was listening to music, worshiping God on the way to the grocery store and I felt Him (in my spirit) say, "If you wouldn't have decided to follow me, today would have been your appointed day to die." I felt and knew it in my heart that it would have been a death of self-destruction because of my choices.

The fear of the Lord adds length to life, but the years of the wicked are cut short.

Proverbs 10:27

I was so thankful that I chose to forsake my self-destructive ways, follow Him, and jump track and go the other way on the narrow road. I don't pretend to understand all the ways of God. All I know is what He has shown and told me. God's way is the only way.

I called to the Lord, who is worthy of praise,

And I am saved from my enemies.

The cords of death entangled me;

The torrents of destruction overwhelmed me;

The cords of the grave coiled around;

The snares of death confronted me.

In my distress I called to the Lord;

I cried to my God for help.

From his temple he heard my voice;

My cry came before him, into His ears.

The earth trembled and quaked,

And the foundations of the mountains shook;

They trembled because He was angry.

Smoke rose from His nostrils;

Consuming fire came from His mouth,

Burning coals blazed out of it.

He parted the heavens and came down;

Dark clouds were under His feet.

He mounted the cherubim and flew;

He soared on the wings of the wind.

He made darkness his covering, His

Canopy around Him—

The dark rain clouds of the sky.

Out of the brightness of His presence clouds advanced,

with hailstones and bolts of lightning.

The Lord thundered from heaven;

The voice of the Most High resounded.

He shot his arrows and scattered the enemies,

Great bolts of lightning and routed them.

The valleys of the sea were exposed

and the foundations of the earth laid

bare at Your rebuke, O Lord,

at the blast of breath from Your nostrils.

He reached down from on high and took hold of me;

He drew me out of the deep waters.

He rescued me from my powerful enemy,

from my foes, who were too strong for me.

Psalms 18: 3-17

    I call forth the warrior heart in all of your women Lord and pray that they would know that they are worth fighting for.

    Rise up, oh mighty woman of God and take your place among the anointed for you were born for such a time as this.

7

TRUE FREEDOM

When I think of freedom, thoughts of a long wooden dock leading out to a deep, blue sea, fills my mind. Freedom to me is the warm, summer sun kissing my face while listening to my children laughing and playing in the nearby creek, or my husband barbequing chicken and corn on the cob while I happily set the outside table, inhaling deeply of the freshly cut sunflower bouquet in the center. I think of lazy spring afternoons snuggled down on the front porch swing with a delicious book, perhaps some chocolate, strawberries and iced lemonade on the side. Freedom to me would mean a life of paid bills, stocked pantries, family vacations, healthy children and all basic needs met. I think of thunderstorms, pouring rain, freshly picked lilacs, white, picket fences, Italian cuisine, dancing the cha-cha in my kitchen while baking double chocolate brownies. Freedom means herb gardens, home-grown yellow and red peppers, squash, green onions, oregano and garlic bread that I make in my bread machine. I image my husband chasing me around the clothesline while I'm trying to hang up the freshly, bleached sheets and him catching me only to steal a sweet, afternoon kiss. Oil paint on canvas, messy hair swept up in a #2 pencil, my imagination running wild, and stroke after stroke stimulates the mindset of freedom.

True freedom for me would be a life well lived.

When my first husband was in prison in Jasper, Florida, our daughter and I went to visit him a few times. Sitting there in the outside courtyard I wondered what it would be like to be stuck behind bars, not able to go to the park with your children, not able to see your children being born, and not able to kiss your spouse every night before bed. You would only feel half alive. You would be breathing but not truly living.

Some people's prisons were laid way back in their childhood. Ask yourself: What do I need to be free from drug addiction, pornography, fear? What holds you back from living the life that you've always dreamt of?

CHOOSING FREEDOM

I found my One True Love. I searched wide and found the One my heart longed for. He took my past and washed me clean. He took my scarlet letter and tore it to pieces and drew me close without hesitation.

I'm here to tell you that you also have that choice! You can be free and live a life that you've only dreamt of. I'm not talking about being rich and famous. I'm talking about having a deep seeded peace and reassurance that you are loved; an understanding that you are valuable, and that God has a plan for your life. I am talking about restoration and redemption. I'm talking about no longer feeling rejected everywhere you go and actually feeling like you belong. I'm talking about looking at your life, seeing little things you often overlook and delighting in them. I'm talking about the freedom to walk down the street knowing you are making the right choices in your family, finances, and life. Having other people smile at you for no reason and having them want to be a part of your life. Having a deep-seeded contentment knowing that you belong to God and He has your life in His hands. I'm talking about being a part of something bigger than just what's going on in your life. I'm talking about being proud of who you are. I am talking about forgiving yourself and accepting and valuing your own body.

The thief comes only to steal and kill and destroy; I have come that they may have life, and have it to the full.

John 10:10

THE KEYS TO FREEDOM

I will give you the keys of the kingdom of heaven; whatever you bind on earth will be bound in heaven and whatever you loose on earth will be loosed in heaven.

Mathew 16:19

Some people don't even realize how incredibly bound they are until they get serious about claiming their freedom. What do you need freedom from? Look closely at your life (even if you have to put the book down for a few minutes) and identify the things that are hindering your walk with God. How do you know what you need to be free from? You need to be free from anything that threatens to destroy your character in any manner. What is it in your life that is threatening to overtake you? Let's look at those things that can hold us in bondage, which can be physical (drugs, alcohol, sexual and self- abuse, etc.), emotional (past, family, abusive partner, etc.), mental (strongholds, mindsets, negative thinking patterns, etc.), and spiritual (the occult, witchcraft, generational curses, word curses, etc.). This list only covers a few examples of the types of bondage that believers can experience and a lot of these can cross over between physical, emotional, mental, and spiritual. I pray over you now that if you are ready to take your first step on that road to freedom, then pray this prayer with me now.

"Jesus, I believe that you are the Christ, I ask you to please forgive me for all the sins that I have committed. I repent of the things that hold me in bondage and ask you to come into my heart to be my Lord and Savior. I ask that You do a deep seeded cleansing of all of my organs and my womb. May they be restored back to life. I ask that You restore all that has been lost or stolen through sexual sins. In Jesus's name, I pray for total freedom from everything in my life that is contrary to your word (the bible) and ways. I ask that you loose the chains of injustice! Thank you for hearing my prayers, Amen."

I have seen people completely delivered from suicidal tendencies, Asthma, drug addiction, self-mutilation, depression, eating disorders, chronic pain, and warts among other hindrances. I have seen wombs be completely restored back to life-giving homes. Just know that Jehovah God is the final authority in every situation you face in your life. Jesus died so we could be forgiven for our sin and healed of our infirmities. By His stripes, we are healed. "Jesus," is the name above all names.

So, if the Son sets you free, you will be free indeed.

John 8:36

As soon as you cry out to God, He comes for you.

I remember when I found total freedom from my past. It was like a huge weight was taken off of me. Even though God had freed me, He did not give the people I knew amnesia about my past for two reasons. First, He just doesn't usually do that. Secondly, He wanted those people to see Him in me and how drastically I had changed. Believe me, it was a drastic change. We cannot change our past and the things we did. However, we can pray that the negative effects of our past, in our lives and others, would be healed and restored.

I found deliverance in many ways. Spending alone time with God was one of the major ways I received deliverance. Another way was through trained Christian counselors. When I found the battle too great to fight on my own, I would ask other God-fearing individuals to pray for me. Word curses also needed to be broken. This was as easy as just speaking out loud "I break each and every agreement I made with the Enemy and word curses against my life. I break this with the blood of Christ, in Jesus's name." After these were broken, I had to line myself up with the word of God. Did my healing happen overnight? No. I had to renew my mind so it would be conformed to the mind of Christ by reading His scripture daily. In order to remain free, I have to choose life instead of death in every choice I make (see *Deuteronomy 30:19*). I have to fight the good fight, put God first in all that I do, and walk in the spirit not allowing my flesh to dictate my decisions (see *Galatians 5:16*). Do I fail? Daily. Do I get back up, ask for forgiveness, and keep going? Daily.

    I know that Christ died for my freedom and it's my responsibility to choose to walk in His ways, daily.

    Stay close to God and soak in His presence. The closer you are to Him, the more freedom you will find. I provide a basic outline on the next few pages for you to start but make sure you don't go it alone.

DEEP CLEANSING

    A few of my girlfriends and I watched a series about spiritual land cleansing. The one thing that was said that really stuck with me was that the demonic (strongholds) come second to sin. First, there must be some form of sin in our lives that opens the door for demonic spirits. I believe this to be true with human cleansing as well. Unforgiveness is a sin that opens the door for strongholds. If we have any unforgiveness towards anyone (including ourselves) God will not forgive us of our sins (see Mathew 6:15). Forgiving others is incredibly serious to God. He sent His son so that we could be forgiven for our sins. He expects us to show the same mercy to others. Like I said, unforgiveness provides a wide open door for the enemy to come in and conquer our souls. When I need to forgive a person, I write them a letter saying that they hurt me, but I have forgiven them. Then, I throw the letter away. If I need to ask someone to forgive me, I write and give a letter to the person that I have hurt. How do we know if we have forgiven someone for their offense towards us? We know that we have forgiven when we only feel compassion towards them whenever we think of them or see them. After we have dealt with any unforgiveness towards other, then we can ask God to forgive our sin. When we do this, our sin is placed under the shed blood of Christ. When we've done all of that, then we can renounce the demonic. Whether you are a long-time Christian or a new Christian, I suggest that you do not go through the process of forgiving others alone. Get another mature Christian to help you. Searching one's heart is a very delicate and precious thing. It is enhanced by sharing it with another understanding heart.

    I know that I make it sound so easy to forgive. I actually had a situation in my life that almost destroyed me. If I wouldn't have chosen to forgive, I would be six feet under right now along with two other people that seriously betrayed me.

I've heard it said that unforgiveness is like drinking poison hoping that the person who hurt you will die. Some of us have serious pains that others have inflicted upon us and we have to make a choice. Either we can learn to live with these wide open, gaping wounds, or we can choose to forgive and be healed of our past.

GUIDELINES FOR DEEP SEEDED CLEANSING AND BREAKTHROUGH

1. Forgive others for anything harmful they did to you
2. Ask Jesus to forgive you of your sins and forgive yourself for your sins
3. Break every word agreement that you made with the enemy
4. Plead the blood of Jesus over your situation
5. Rebuke a harassing spirit firmly in the Mighty name of Jesus!!!
6. Praise Jehovah, exalt Him, and place Him back on the throne in your life!
7. Call forth a triple hedge of protection around you and your family daily (this is the hedge that protected Job before God allowed Satan to test him).
8. Call forth warring and guardian angels to protect, and war for you and your family, home, work, etc.
9. Praise God always and continually for everything in your life!!!

It is for freedom that Christ has set us free. Stand firm, then, and do not let yourselves be burdened again by a yoke of slavery.

Galatians 5:1

There is a time for everything, and a season for every activity under heaven:

A time to be born and a time to die,

A time to plant and a time to uproot,

A time to kill and a time to heal

A time to tear down and a time to build,

A time to weep and a time to laugh,

A time to mourn and a time to dance,

A time to scatter stones and a time to gather them,

A time to embrace and a time to refrain,

A time to search and a time to give up,

A time to keep and a time to throw away,

A time to tear and a time to mend,

A time to be silent and a time to speak,

A time to love and a time to hate, A time for war and a time for peace,

Ecclesiastes 3: 1-8

Now is my time to speak!

On this day, I speak FREEDOM to you.

On this day, I say to you, you will find freedom. You will no longer be in chains hiding in the prison of your mind.

On this day, the wall that separates you from your purpose is coming down. On this day, I speak life and peace into your being; a peace that surpasses all understanding. I tell you that salvation and eternal life can be yours through Jesus Christ. You will rise up and no longer dwell in the shadows. You will find the treasures that are within. You will walk in love and turn the key to open the door so others will follow you on this journey. You will no longer be conformed to the image of this world; you will no longer wallow in the mud. Rather, you can call out to the One who created you, be washed in His love, restored and reconciled to your rightful position in Him, have a crown placed on your head and lifted to higher ground.

I speak it out right now through my words and as you are reading this page the power of God will come upon you. His warring and guardian angels will watch over and surround you. I call forth a refire in your faith and ask Him to stir that fire in your heart. It is by no accident that you hold this book in your hands.

You have been bound for too long, Chosen One, it is time for you to pick up your sword and fight for your freedom!

PART 3

UNVEILING OUR TRUE IDENTITY

IDENTITY

Who are we exactly?

We can get our identity in many different ways. We can get it through: the words our mother and father speak over us when we are in the womb; the way our parents treat us or speak to us or speak about us; our family's history or reputation in our community; our teachers if they stereotype us as smart kids or stupid kids or perhaps "hopeless" kids; and from our peers or classmates.

Our identity is pretty much whatever we want to accept as the truth about ourselves. Whether that truth is a lie or not, if we choose to accept it, it becomes our personal truth. I received my identity from a number of things. First, when my dad never came for me I believed that I was not worth fighting for let alone worthy to be loved. Second, the harsh words that were spoken over me made me believe that I was a waste of space, not worth the air that I was breathing. Third, some of my teachers made me believe that I was very ignorant and behind in class. I was frequently the stupid kid who had to sit in the front of the class and wear the dunce cap. I was the kid who couldn't concentrate in class and got tested for dyslexia. When the test results came back negative, it just "proved" that I was just stupid. I flunked all of my tests and my dog usually ate my homework. I came to school dirty and left ashamed. I had an aunt who constantly heaped shame on me. "Shame on you," was her reply to so many things that I did. My stepdad told me repeatedly that I was dumber than a box of rocks and that I wasn't going to amount to anything. Different family members believed that if my mom allowed me to go to high school that I would end up knocked up and flunk out of school. I had begun to believe that I was too sexy, too stupid, unworthy, vain, dirty, ignorant, foolish, and I usually had "no clue what I was talking about."

SIMPLY ME

False identity is sometimes extremely hard to overcome when we have accepted it our whole lives. Before I could even see the real me, I had to first leave the small town that gave me those labels and figure out who I was. Layer by layer, the lies about who I was eventually came to light. Underneath all of those layers, I found the true me and I realized that I was lovely, smart, worthy, full of character, somewhat wise, and what I had to say was just as important as the next person. I also learned how to wash my clothes and make them smell good, and take care of myself. I learned that I loved: to paint vibrant abstract pictures on canvas; read facts and relational books; the smell of the ocean and the warm sand under my feet; to dance in the Florida rain; drink iced Pepsi and all kinds of food (I really don't have a favorite food). I learned that I: am gentle and have a giving and kind spirit; feel immensely for those who do not have their basic needs met; love moonlight and the smell of the sweet, Montana breeze;

love the smell of salt water, fresh deep fried crab legs, and the sounds of soft Reggie music coming from the beach; and I like to body surf. My favorite flower is the sunflower because of its vast, brilliant, and brightly colored. I love warm bubble baths and the smell of my children's little piggies. Through life, I have learned a lot of different things about myself that I would have never known if I hadn't started peeling off the layers. My identity has changed so much from when I was a young woman. I went on a path of self-discovery and discovered my true self and the woman that I was created to be underneath all those layers. I love to write books and watch my children as they laugh and play together. I enjoy seeing my children develop their own talents. I love it when my children are happy and well taken care of. I love me. I love the woman who was under all those lies, curses, confusion, and pain. Today, I am content with who I see in the mirror. Do I still have things to discover? Yes, but that is part of the journey.

We *can* find ourselves in this sea of delusion if we choose to look through the eyes of the One who formed our tiny, little selves and planted the treasures that lie within us. When we see ourselves through the eyes of our Maker, we will be surprised at how fearfully and wonderfully He created us to be. We are the treasures hidden in the darkness. For once, we find out who we truly are and what our purpose and mission is in this life. We become irrevocably committed to our true destiny. We are precious and irreplaceable. There's only one of me so I plan to be the best me I can be.

      We are the essence of beauty and worth because we are loved by our Creator. He placed different attributes and aspects of Himself into each and every one of us. Through life's journey, we will find who we are and what we have been created for.

"All the days ordain for me were written in your book before one of them came to be."

Psalms 139: 16

8

BATTLE SCARS

SLAYING DRAGONS

If one stands alone, she still stands…

As the smoke bellows over the battlefield, the sting of silence echoes loudly through her ears. She wonders if she is still alive. Did she survive the great battle? She looks down and sees her blood-sodden boots and sword still in hand. The great dragon has been defeated! He lies in a helpless mound at her feet. Her Father and his men frantically search for her among the slain. They fear the great dragon has consumed her. They hear metal scraping the ground as she slowly pulls up her sword, and turns around to go back for the others. Her Father looks up with tears in his eyes fearing her loss. The smoke clears and there she stands, in full armor, long blond hair, matted with sweat from her freshly removed helmet. She stands alone, yet she still stands with the slain dragon at her feet. The warriors also taste the legendary victory coming out of the hills. As the smoke clears and all others are gone, she stands in the strength of her Father, the King. Some of the warriors doubted her abilities to make it through this great battle. They watched and made bets as to how long she would last before she cowered. But, she knew in her heart this victory was hers. Her Father's belief in her gave her the courage to keep fighting. The warriors stood still as she realized her great victory. She straightened her back and stood tall knowing well what she had just claimed. As the warriors waited in awe, she raised her sword "VICTORY IS OURS!" The sounds of triumph echoed through the treetops consuming the battlegrounds. Her Father had never been as proud as he was in this very moment.

If we could only see the great battles that are being warred on our behalf in the heavens, we would be overwhelmed. Through the eye of the spirit, I have seen a glimpse of some of the battles that have been fought for me. Every day, every decision, every word is a battle waiting to be won.

There are great battles in our lives that we fight sometimes for years. Some battles we fear may consume us, yet we continue to fight.

Let me encourage you that if your Father, the King has already told you that the battle has been won, then claim that battle as your own and stand firm on God's words until you see the victory manifest before your eyes.

When the winds rage and the sea is roaring and you think that your situation is going to overtake you, step back and ask God for peace in the eye of that storm. Hurricane winds may rage all around you, but if you dwell in the eye where your Prince of Peace is, there you will find rest.

My God has fought many battles for me. Sometimes, He tells me to pick up my sword. Other times, He tells me to take up my position and just praise Him. On some occasions, He tells me to be still and know that He is God. To stand back and watch the long arm of the Lord war for me.

In order to wage war on one's enemy, we must first understand who we are and what power we have access to.

As a daughter of the King, I am co-heir with Jesus. In death and in life, the Prince has given me full authority over all the power of the enemy. However, without the wisdom and the knowledge to know how to use that authority and armor, I am as good as dead.

For one, as daughters of the King, we must understand that we are fully armed and dangerous to the enemy. Our enemy fears the day that we come of age and learn how to fight for our rights and for our kingdom. We have the power through the resurrection to speak forth life or death. We have the power to heal the blind and make the lame to walk. We have the power to raise the dead (see Mathew 10:6-8). We have the power over all the schemes of our enemy. Because we have victory through the resurrection of Jesus, we must start fighting as though this battle has already been won.

This war is not for the faint of heart. It is for those who know who they are and Who they belong to. Our battles can only be won when we truly believe what our Father has taught us. Victory occurs when we understand that, although we are afraid, we can face giants and slay them if we truly know that our Father never loses the battles He fights on our behalf. We have to know Who's got our back. We have to know that our Father, the King is a Mighty Warrior.

We must read the end of the book and know who wins the war. Will we encounter loss? Yes. Will we be wounded? Yes. Will there be casualties? Yes. Will it be worth it? Yes!!!

I once heard a song by Misty Edwards that rang out into one of my many battles, "If you don't quit, you'll win!"

Daily, we must rise. Daily, we must position our mind. Daily, we must put on our armor. Daily we must know when our feet hit the floor, hell trembles.

We must proclaim fearlessness. We must speak fearlessly. We must walk by faith. Our footprints must lead others into victory. We must understand that our time here is short and every second of every day counts.

We must wage war fearlessly and ride into the pits of hell to rescue those who are bound in chains. We must understand that the only power our enemy has over us is the power WE give him. The only access our enemy has to our lives is the doors that we open for him, by our thoughts and choices.

We must understand that we are *more* than conquers.

No, in all these things we are more than conquerors through him who loved us.

Romans 8:37

Mighty Women of God, let us stop losing the battles that we face in this life, shall we; the battles of bulimia, perversion, depression, fear, anxiety, suicidal thoughts, adultery, and shame, etc. Let us learn to win the battles of self-worth and self-hate. Let us equip ourselves to war victoriously. Every day we must learn to get out of bed in the morning and put on our armor. To not only put it on but to learn how to use it. There are many great books you can purchase regarding the armor of God. A good one that I am reading now is Lisa Bevere's book Girls with Swords. The armor of God will be found in the ancient book in Ephesians.

"Finally, be strong in the Lord and in His mighty power. Put on the full armor of God so that you can take your stand against the devil's schemes. For our struggle is not against flesh and blood, but against the spiritual forces of evil in the heavenly realms. Therefore put on the full armor of God, so that when the day of evil comes, you may be able to stand your ground, and after you have done everything, to stand. Stand firm then, with the <u>belt of truth</u> buckled around your waist, with the <u>breastplate of righteousness</u> in place and with your <u>feet fitted</u> with the readiness that comes from the <u>gospel of peace</u>. In addition to all this, take up the <u>shield of faith</u>, with which you can extinguish all the flaming arrows of the evil one. Take the <u>helmet of salvation</u> and the <u>sword of the Spirit</u>, which is the word of God. And <u>pray in the Spirit</u> on all occasions with all kinds of prayers and requests. With this in mind, be alert and always keep on praying for all saints.

Ephesians 6:10

THE UNRELENTING CHAINS OF FEAR

I once sat in the claustrophobic darkness of bondage in which fear of abandonment was my closest "friend."

I'm going to share a little bit of how my life was before I found freedom from the fear of abandonment.

Fear-false evidence that appears real in order to get you to follow your emotions. (This is a quote that I heard when I was watching Joyce Meyer one morning).

When I got married to James I had no self-worth. I put my husband in the place of both of my dad's and every other male role model in my life who didn't give me what I needed. I then demanded that my husband fill every empty hole in me. That was a big mistake. I was so afraid that my husband was going to abandon me that I would push him away just knowing that someday he would leave like my daddy did.

I was so afraid of this that I would yell at him if he came home twenty minutes late from work. If I even thought that he was looking or even glancing at another woman, I would yell at him and accuse him of not loving me. It would make me feel like I wasn't good enough. I believed that someday he was going to leave me for someone better. I just knew it.

He is our Father in the sight of God, in whom he believed-the God who gives life to the dead and calls those things that are not as though they were.

Romans 4: 1/2 17

My heart is stirred by a noble theme as I recite my verses for the king; my tongue is the pen of a skillful writer.

Psalms 45:1

We must choose our words very carefully.

The tongue has the power of life and death, and those who love it will eat its fruit.

Proverbs 18:21

By the words we think and speak we can either call those things out in the positive realm or in the negative realm. Fear has a funny way of trying to steal our destiny through our words. I've seen fear steal so many purposes by putting thoughts into a person's mind that makes them fearful and act on fear instead of God's truth.

As the rain and snow come down from heaven, and do not return to it without watering the earth and making it bud and flourish, so that it yields seed for the sower and bread for the eater, so is my word that goes out from my mouth. It will accomplish what I desire and achieve the purpose for which I sent it.

Isaiah 55:10&11

Our words determine our destiny.

Fear is to Satan as faith is to God.

    I submitted to fear for so many years. I have no clue why my husband stayed with me for so long. A thought would come into my mind then I would accept it as the truth. Then, I would accuse James of whatever thought the enemy had put into my mind. I wasted so many years going in circles this way.

    Fear became such a huge part of my life that I was dependent on it. I did not know how to live without it.

    I remember one time at a woman's revival when the preacher lady cast fear out of me. I felt so unnerved and I kept thinking, "Wow, now what?" I felt empty, like a major part of me had just left. I actually felt abandoned by losing fear, if that makes sense. Of course, it came back and this time seven times greater (see Luke 11:25). I had gone to many counseling sessions to get free from the debilitating effects of the fear of abandonment in my life. Finally, I realized the only way to get rid of my fear was to face it head-on. So I wrote my fear out. "So, what if my second husband leaves me for another woman and I am then left alone at ground zero, again." And then I would allow myself to go through the pain of that instance? I would convince myself that it will be completely overwhelming and heartbreaking but eventually, I would learn to pull myself out of bed and put one foot in front of the other. I would learn to exhale until one day I wouldn't have to remind myself to breathe again. I convinced myself that time would heal me and one day I would have forgotten the shape of his lips and facial hair. Sometime later I would have forgotten the manliness of his hands and the way he wore his hair. Years later I would have forgotten the way he held me close and soon enough I would have forgotten his smell. For some reason doing this gave me a sense of closer and peace.

After I road that fear all the way out, I then wrote every scripture that I could find regarding the opposite of fear (faith) on index cards and used those scriptures to speak out against fear. I would believe in faith that God had delivered me from fear and that I was strong and courageous. I went around and around with this. I would choose the truth a few times and then accept the lies and blow up on my husband. At one point I actually thought that I would never get free from the root of fear and I would just lose my mind. I had to learn not to accept those thoughts as the truth and choose to keep doing what I was doing and not react to the fear.

I would often say to my husband, "What you do with your life is your choice. Someday, I will stand before God and give an account of my own life and I will stand alone. I will not be able to blame you for my mistakes or shortcomings."

I had to continually remind myself that my husband was only a man and not a god. He could not fill me the way God filled me.

I had no clue that fear could make me feel abandoned. I always thought that fear meant that you were afraid to proclaim Christ. Or, that you would hide in the corner like a wallflower, not wanting to be seen. That was not me.

This is how a typical day would go for me when I was bound by the fear of abandonment. A negative thought would come into my mind that seemed so real that I would accept it as the truth and act upon it. These thoughts always had to do with my feelings and how abandoned I would feel if these thoughts were true, which I believed to be the case. Now, I'm a visionary kind of girl. When these thoughts would start running through my mind, I would have a vision that was so real that it was like watching a movie in my head. These thoughts would become reality to me.

Let me give you an example. In 2008, my husband was working at the family meat shop as a butcher. I was at home washing dishes. I was just standing in the kitchen minding my own business and the children were sitting at the dining room table doing their school work. Then, suddenly I had a thought: "Remember when your husband didn't answer the phone last night when he was at work? Well, that's because he was with another woman. Remember how that excuse he gave you was so lame that you thought that he was lying? Well, that's because he was. Remember how you saw so and so drive by around the same time? That's because she was going to the shop to see him. Don't be naive or you are going to get left, again." As soon as I heard these thoughts, my head came up and my back straightened out. Before I knew it, "Dirty Dog," came out of my mouth. The children were loaded into my suburban and off to the meat shop as fast as my suburban would go. All the while, this vile vision replayed in my mind. When I think back now, all I can picture is Cruella De Vil, going Mach 20 with her hair on fire driving like a mad woman, suburban loaded down with screaming kids and fire coming out of the tailpipes. Dust storming as my breaks screeched to an abrupt stop in the shop parking lot. I jumped out of the suburban, ran into the shop, and asked to see my husband outside, immediately. Then, I tore into him, not even once giving him the benefit of the doubt or even asking him if what I saw in my vision was true. (You have to understand these thoughts happened years before my husband had even thought about having an affair.) My thoughts and vision seemed so real. I just knew my womanly intuition was telling me the vision was accurate. Most of the time, I would find out that my vision was completely inaccurate and none of the events that the spirit of fear had placed into my mind were true but the emotions that went along with them felt very real.

The enemy would feed me a lie; I would accept it as the truth then act upon it, causing total chaos in our marriage and family.

I think back and cringe at how many times I demanded that my husband give me a full account of where he was, what he was doing, and who he was with. This was not an isolated event. This went on for YEARS! I was a prisoner of fear; fear of rejection and fear of abandonment. I have no clue why my husband stayed with me. Satan knew that it would hurt me deeply and devastate me if James ever rejected me, especially after I swore that I would never let another man into my heart. Looking back now, Satan was wrong. It did not destroy me when my husband chose to betray me with another woman. It freed me. After agreeing with fear and falsely accusing my husband for YEARS, the ultimate onslaught of fear and abandonment took place. My husband had an affair. When I realized my behavior and what my husband had done, my bleeding heart burst inside of my chest and out poured the entire brokenness from every childhood wound and loss. For a year and a half, my heart inflicted pain and destruction on everyone around me. I cut off anyone I thought would threaten or stab my heart again. I excluded myself from all public affairs. I wanted to run away from the pain but I couldn't run away from myself. I wanted to run away, period. The only thing I wanted was God. I knew He could heal me. I kept asking my husband to move us to another state away from all those around us. I felt like they were the ones inflicting the pain. I wanted to run and hide. A few nights, I even wanted to give up and die. The pain was so much more than I felt I could handle. I kept crying out to God and telling Him that I could not take it anymore. My heart was bleeding more than it had ever. The scars were being lanced open, the scabs from the past picked, and the tenderness exposed. God kept telling me "There is no other way, the only way is through. You must go through; your healing awaits you on the other side." So, I mustered up the little bit of strength that I had and moved forward one day, one hour, one second at a time.

    I married a good man. But, because of my calloused heart, poor self-image, and my captive mind, I pushed him away and he chose to become a man that I did not even know. By professing I was a Christian and acting the way I did, my husband wanted nothing to do with my God. Our family life was a mess.

    Finally, the healing began to take place. James and I had gone to see a prophet that told me I had a spirit of timidity. I looked it up in the dictionary at my sister's house, dropped off the children at school, and headed out to the reservoir near our town where I pitched a tent and eagerly sought healing. God met me there and directed me to 2 Timothy 1:7.

For God did not give us a spirit of timidity, but a spirit of power, of love and of self-discipline

2 Timothy 1:7

At that point, God revealed to me that I was a fearful person. It was at my campsite that God exposed the dark places in my mind. My older sister texted scripture to me while I was laying on the bed in my canvas temple, listening to the waves crashing along the shoreline. I needed to identify the lies that Satan was telling me and take every thought captive by the renewing of my mind; whatever things are true...think on these things. Even after much deliverance, I kept choosing to let fear control me and invade my thoughts. My husband decided to leave the marriage throughout this time. I would get some deliverance and he would come back- thinking everything was going to be OK, but it was not. Something would happen that would make me afraid and fear would take over. I was completely controlled by it. The last time my husband came back home he left his wedding ring on the window sill. A confrontation took place and I ended up leaving our home. When I returned, the fear was so great that my husband and I could not stop fighting. He gave his life back to God while the children and I were away. My mind, on the other hand, was so full of fear because my ultimate fear had become a reality. I had been replaced. My fear had been proven to be true, I was not worth loving. It was at this time that God called me to a 40-day fast. The enemy was trying to completely destroy me through this devastating blow. I fully submitted myself to God. God pulled these lies out by the roots.

Submit yourself, then, to God, resist the devil and he will flee from you.

James 4:7

After my fast, I was able to consistently agree with God's word. Now, if something comes into my mind that does not line up with the word of God, it gets thrown out, immediately. Every day, I choose freedom.

James and I tried to save our marriage, but that's another story....

Another thing that greatly helped me to get free from fear was God's personal promises. Through this time in our marriage, I went to a lot of prayer meetings seeking strength and help to deal with the events that were taking place. At those meetings, God would promise me things through prophecy or a word of knowledge given by other believers. If I felt these promises resonated with my spirit, then I would cling to them. Anytime the spirit of fear tried to enter my mind, I would speak out one of those promises and place my trust in God and not in fear.

I have made an outline to guide you through this time of bondage into your own personal freedom. I am zealous for you to find the same kind of freedom that I found through Jesus. I completely understand what it is like to struggle under the weight of a spiritual bully.

BREAKING THE CHAINS

1. <u>Identify wrong thinking</u>. I did not know I had a problem until I was prayed over. I honestly believed that the way I thought was just how I was supposed to think.

> a. If you think that you might have a stronghold, but can't put your finger on it, ask you're pastor, elder, mentor, or your spouse to pray with you and seek God's council.

2. <u>Pick up your sword</u> (the word of God is like a double-edged sword), and use it to slay wrong thinking patterns.

a. If you feel week, find another prayer warrior or two that will stand by your side as you fight this stronghold.
b. Remember your sword is the word of God. Take out your bible and speak scripture (regarding your faith or fearing not) over your life and to the spirit of fear. God had me dwell in the book of Joshua for some time to convince me that I was strong and courageous. Ask him if that's where He would have you read.

3. <u>Implant truth into your mind</u>
    a. Memorize God's word, and meditate on it day and night. Speak freedom scriptures over your mind. Speak out God's personal promises. Call forth prophecies that were spoken over you. Does that sound crazy? Try it; you have nothing to lose.
    b. Ask God to replace the opposite spirit. Negative and positive thought patterns cannot dwell in your mind at the same time. When the negative is uprooted ask God to replace it with His opposite. Faith in exchange for fear, love for hate, purity for perversion etc.
    c. I wrote down every scripture (counteracting fear) that God gave me on index cards. I read those scriptures out loud every morning. The truth of God's word WILL set you free. Don't give up!

4. <u>Fasting enhances your prayers greatly</u>! Because fear had guided me my entire life, I believed an intense fast was necessary. Pray and seek God's guidance on when and

how long to fast. There have been times that God asked me to just fast from foods that bring death; to eat only life-giving foods (the Daniel Fast). This kind of fast helped me to be cautious of the choices that I made between life and death, in my food, words, thoughts, etc.

(This guideline holds the same theory to be true when dealing with many different hindrances and not just the fear of abandonment).

If what you are thinking does not line up with the word of God, then it is not coming from God. Just remember that God is love and God's perfect love casts out all fear. So, if the thought coming into your mind starts with "What if" and is accompanied by the feeling of being afraid, it's probably not from God. Everything starts in the mind: life, dreams, ambitions, wants, desires, and temptations. Think about that. What doesn't start in the mind? If you are to be an overcomer in this lifetime, you must first master your mind. In the morning before your day begins, order your day. Speak over your day that "Fear is expecting something bad to happen, but on THIS day I wholeheartedly expect great things to take place."

No one will be able to stand up against you all the days of your life. As I was with Moses, so I will be with you; I will never leave you nor forsake you.

Joshua 1:5

If God is for us, who can be against us?

Romans 8:31

I sought the Lord, and he answered me; He delivered me from all my fears.

Psalms 34:4

Finally, be strong in the Lord and in His mighty power.

Ephesians 6:10

You are worth fighting for….

9
TREASURES IN DARKNESS

I will go before you and will level the mountains; I will break down gates of bronze and cut through bars of iron, I will give you the treasures of darkness, riches stored in secret places, so that you may know that I am the Lord, the God of Israel, who summons you by name.

Isaiah 45:2&3

We *are* God's treasures that have been hidden in the darkness for far too long. We are the diamonds, amethysts and emeralds of the Most High. He created us and we are His most treasured possessions.

Ladies, imagine how you would feel if your fiancé, husband, or boyfriend surprised you with a trip to New York City, took you to the Tiffany's on 5th Ave. and told you to pick any rock in the entire company. Just image for a second how that would make you feel. I know that I would be having a really, great day.

God looked over the whole world at His beautiful jewels and chose YOU and me out of all of the other entire gems in the selection. Like I said, if you're reading this book, you have been chosen. You and I were hand-picked by God to represent Him in this life. Underneath all that darkness we are beautiful flawless treasures. If you ask God, He will tell you the exact gem that you are. God told me one time that I was His blue diamond. All I could think of was the heart of the ocean. I looked up blue diamond and found out that a blue diamond is the rarest and most valuable of all diamonds.

God has so many blue diamonds that are just waiting to be uncovered, washed off and polished to perfection.

I was clueless when different people in our church would tell me "You need to know who you are in Christ." For the life of me I had no clue what that meant. Sometimes when I was doing my bible study I would write, "Knowing who you are in Christ." Then I would draw a blank.

Several years ago, I had an abscess tooth for over two years. I went to the dentist and he couldn't pull it out. He tried twice with no avail. God had been prompting me to go to the Tuesday night "soaking in God's presence" service, for healing. Every Tuesday there was always an excuse. "The kids are dirty," "dinner is not ready," "I have no babysitter for the baby," etc., etc., etc. One sunny, summer day I took my girls and two other girls to the water park in a different town. My baby was with the sitter and it just so happened to be a Tuesday. We drove by the church-half wet and in our swimsuits and sweat pants, and hair all windblown with no make-up on. I knew I had to stop. I had the girls play outside and everyone in the church prayed for me for about an hour. A few of them prophesied over me. It was good. On that night, I found out who I was in Christ, namely: (I feel like a lot of these things are universal for God's children. For a lot of these feel free to apply them to yourself, personally)

I am a worthy child of the Most High God.

-I am a princess and one day will rule and reign with God

-I am highly favored among women

-God wants to give me the desires of my hearts

-My voice and words will be healing instruments for all who hear them

-I am the Lord's redeemed child

-I am cherished by God

-God is going to glorify me and in so doing He will be glorified

-A teacher to women, because of all that I have been through

-I am climbing a mountain and I am almost to the top

-When I reach the top, there will be a field of daisies

- When at the top, I will turn around and praise God for what He has delivered me from!

-A worshiper of God

-A fighting soldier of God

-A commanding officer

-A spiritual giant

-God has given me the authority to deliver those that are in the same bondage that I was in

-not a quitter

-God Himself is warring on my behalf

-If God is for me, who can come against me

-I have received the resurrection power

-I believe that God is moving me into a position of authority

- I've been set apart

-I've been called by name

-A powerful instrument in the hands of God

-A woman of noble character

-God has filled me with His love

-No longer have to survive in the desert

-living in the thriving lush gardens of God's love

-My children rise up and call me blessed

-A dancer before the King

-A fresh water cistern

-An ambassador to The Most High God

- The Holy Temple of God

- enthusiastic

- having zeal

-taking back the ground that the enemy has taken

-A fighter for the freedom of those in bondage

-Free

This is who I am in Christ. This is who we are in Christ!

This describes the woman that I was made to be, before I was formed in my mother's womb. This is what God had in mind. No longer will I be conformed to this world and molded to the "self-image" that was implanted into me as a child.

We live in this world, but we are not of this world.

We are holy and anointed, heirs to the throne, Daughters of The King, Mighty Warriors of The Most High God.

I believe that God has a set of blueprints for every person that He creates. I believe that time and circumstances try to change these plans. However, I know from experience that you can get back to those blueprints if you are desperate enough. Spend time in God's presence and little by little you will become who you were formed to be. Little by little you will bust out of this cemented mold that you have been poured into.

In my case, I kept hearing God say, "Go back to your roots." I kept hesitating and saying, "I don't want to go back there, God. There is nothing there but darkness." "You must," He would say and so I did. I traveled back in time in my mind and found that my heart had been held captive by, situations, disappointments, fears, words and circumstances. It was then that I knew my mission .To free my heart from my past. So, I fought the darkness on behalf of my heart. I pulled out the sword of the spirit and spoke scripture over time, circumstance, situation and disappointments and freed my heart. I placed it back in my chest and brought it back with me to the present in order to live, love and be free. It was then that I realized my childhood dreams and character had been lost and forgotten for decades. It was then that I could love and appreciate the small things; it was then that God restored my innocence and a new day was born.

I want to encourage you, if you were like I was and have no clue who you are in Christ seek Him and the closer you get to Him the closer you will get to the real you, the you that God created you to be underneath all of the worldly clothing that you have been forced to wear.

WHO AM I TO YOU LORD?

As I flopped into my recliner, angry at myself for another late, rushed morning, trying to get my children off to school, I opened the book "Waking the Dead" by John Eldredge. I'm immediately hiking through the Weminuche

Wilderness with Eldredge and asking myself the questions, *"What do You think of me, God? Who am I to You?"*

As I could hear my husband playing with the baby in our bedroom and packing for Colorado, I quietly whisper two rooms away, "What do you think of me, God? Who am I to You?"

"Joan of Arc:"   Warrior, fighter, commander.

Just like Eldredge, I too need this heroic title to keep me in the fight.

If you do not know who you are in Christ, seek and ye shall find, knock and the door shall be opened unto you.

When you finally realize who you are in Christ, it is then that you can say (as Hagar did);

"I have now seen the One who sees me "Genesis 16:13 -Lahai Roi- (The God who sees me, hears my cries and delivers me from my powerful enemies).

Have I not commanded you? "Be strong and courageous, do not be terrified; do not be discouraged, for the Lord your God will be with you wherever you go."   *Joshua 1:9*

"Do not let this Book of the Law depart from your mouth; meditate on it day and night, so that you may be careful to do everything written in it. Then you will be prosperous and successful."

Joshua 1:8

No one will be able to stand up against you all the days of your life. As I was with Moses so shall I be with you; I will never leave you or forsake you."

Joshua 1:5

"Get yourself ready! Stand up and say to them, Today I have made you a fortified city, an iron pillar and a bronze wall to stand against the whole land-against kings of Judah, its officials, its priests and the people of the land. They will fight against you but will not overcome you, for I am with you and I will rescue you," declares the Lord.

Jeremiah 1:17-19

"You are a crown of splendor in the Lord's hand, a royal diadem in the hand of your God"

Isaiah 62:3

"Son of man, go now to the house of Israel and speak my words to them."

Ezekiel 3:4

"Son of man I have made you a watchman for the house of Israel; so hear the word I speak and give them warning from me."

Ezekiel 3:17

JOURNAL   2009

    I woke up this morning around 5:45 to answer the phone. My husband and his friend where going to get firewood. After seeing my husband off I made myself some Chai tea and watched the rain and the leaves fall onto the deck. I looked out the kitchen window, standing in my robe and could see the first morning light. I felt God calling me into his presence. I got my bible and notebook off my desk and glanced at my sleepy, little man who was snuggled in the autumn colored quilt that his Grandma had made for James and me, before our wedding day. Not wanting to awaken the two year old ninja, I decided to meet God at the dining room table I sipped some more of my warm Chai tea as I heard the thunder roll. I opened my bible up to the psalms and read the verse "The voice of the Lord strikes with flashes of lightning." Psalm 29:7. I said, "Speak to me oh Lord, let me here thy voice." (I think I used the word "thy" from this Amish devotional, James had been reading to me every night that month.) How great You are, My King. How great is Your unfailing love and your instruction is sugar to my soul. Shout for joy all the earth for the God of Israel still reigns!!!!

As I was reading this scripture, it dawned on me that the vision that I had in church (which I shared in the beginning of this book) took place inside of an old ancient ruin. I saw a beautiful ancient, circular ruin. As I walked closer, I saw a vast, lush garden, filled with bright, radiant colorful flowers and greenery. In the middle of the ruin was a swing with green vines weaved up the ropes with little white flowers on them. There were two huge angels in the garden, one on each side of the swing. On the swing was a giggly, little, blonde haired girl, smiling and swinging ever so freely.

I didn't understand some of the vision so I asked God about it. OK. God, I understand the ruins (they resemble my life). I understand the lush garden that is Your life in me but who is the little girl? God replied, "The little girl is you; I'm fixing to restore you back to innocence."

In the midst of the lightning storm, God spoke to me this morning. "I will rebuild your ancient ruins and restore the places in your heart that have been long devastated."

They will rebuild the ancient ruins and restore the places long devastated; they will renew the ruined cities that have been devastated for generations.

Isaiah 61:4

"In the vision that I gave to you, the garden was an ancient ruin that has been devastated for a long time, since you were around 5. This ruin started depleting around this time. So instead of being watered, so you could grow properly, you were misplaced. Thinking that you were a weed, you were thrown out. You've been trying to survive in the desert. You were cut down, cut up, stomped on, smashed, and yet you still survived. I am so proud of you for surviving. You are a survivor and you don't give up. I sat back and watched, angrily as this happened to you, wanting so desperately to help but you did not cry out to Me. You were not taught to cry out to me. When you did come to Me, you were so sick and weak and almost destroyed. My heart bled when I picked you out of the desert rocks, but now, my child you are allowing Me to nourish you and love you and teach you and water you. And soon you will be healed and will be thriving like a beautiful rose bush planted in the well watered garden of a lush vineyard. I love the fact that you now belong to Me and I can protect you and care for you and guard you from all who try to crush and damage you. You belong to Me and I promise I will always take the very best care of you. I will not stomp you out. You will be glorified and so radiant and I will get the glory for taking charge over your withered, little, lifeless self and creating you into being all that I wanted you to be from the beginning. All that I had planted you to be. I will be your Gardener and I will be a Gardener like none other. I will not leave you to the wolves. I will not leave you for the wild beast to overtake you. I will not allow the hail storms or any other acts of violence to overtake you. With Me always by you and near you, you will be called beautiful, blessed, glorified, at peace, full of love, laughter and light." Your home will be envied by all who come into it because My glory will dwell in your home. I will decorate my temple and you will please Me and I you. Together we will be Super-Natural and all will come to see what I have done through you and with you. You will be lovely and your time of weeping will come to an end. I will restore all that was lost, all that you should have had in the beginning." ~Jehovah.

Who can possibly argue with that? I had no clue that God loved and cherished me so much. I look forward to the day of dancing.

My God is faithful and fulfills His promises. I wanted to share with you just how awesome my God is and how He promised me that He would restore me and He did. I am here today whole hearted and thriving on the promises of God. So many times through this healing process I wanted to give up. So many times I felt the road became too steep and too rough to climb. And, sometimes the terrain did become too extreme for me to keep going and it was in that time God told me to just be still and hold on to Him and when I was ready then we would take another step, together.

GREAT EXPECTATIONS

A wife of noble character who can find?
She is worth far more than rubies.
Her husband has full confidence in her
        and lacks nothing of value.
She brings him good, and not harm, all the days of her life.
She selects wool and flax
        and works with eager hands.
She is like the merchant ships,
        bringing her food from afar.
She gets up while it is still dark;
She provides food for her family
        and portions for her servant girls.
She considers a field and buys it;
        out of her earnings she plants a vineyard.
She sets about her work vigorously;
Her arms are strong for her tasks.
She sees that her trading is profitable,
        and her lamp does not go out at night.
In her hand she holds the distaff
        and grasps the spindle with her fingers.
She opens her arms to the poor
        and extends her hands to the needy.
When it snows, she has no fear for her household;
For all of them are clothed in scarlet.
She makes linen garments and sells them,
        and supplies the merchants with sashes.
She is clothed with strength and dignity;
She can laugh at the days to come.

She speaks with wisdom,
  and faithful instruction is on her tongue.
She watches over the affairs of her household
  and does not eat the bread of idleness.
Her children arise and call her blessed;
Her husband also, and he praises her:
Many women do noble things,
  but you surpass them all."
Charm is deceptive, and beauty is fleeting;
  but a woman who fears the Lord is to be praised.
Give her the reward that she has earned,
  and let her works bring her praise at the city gate.

Proverbs 31:10-31

I have to say that when I first became a Christian I felt like I fell so short of all the other "godly women." I used to get so incredibly embarrassed trying to live up to the standard set by other women. A lot of them had a certain idea of how a Christian woman should be.

A proverbs 31 woman is intimidating not because of any other reason except she sets the standard high and everyone around her knows (through her life song) what she stands for, lives for, and expects out of her life and children.

Growing up, I would rather have been outside building forts or trying to create a time machine out of all the bicycle parts my stepdad brought home from the dump rather than being inside learning how to cook and sew. I loved the outdoors. Don't get me wrong, I loved helping my mom in the garden and harvesting the apples and plums. But, being stuck in an ankle-length wool skirt and forced to be domesticated was not my cup of tea. I prefer strong coffee over tea, anyhow. I was deemed a failure not only in my own eyes but in the eyes of those who thought the idea of a good wife was one who cooked gourmet dinners and whose houses where spick and span. Some of these women were so prideful that they judged their worth based on how clean their houses were or by having dinner ready every night at the same time. I watched as some of their husbands sought understanding elsewhere. I absolutely did not fit into the mold that I was trying to be shoved into. It didn't matter how hard I tried to keep my house clean or how well I cooked dinner, I was just never good enough. My dinners weren't as good as those other women's, my house was not as organized as those other women's, and my children did not always have their homework done the next day. For so many years I tried to live up to the standard that was set for me by other women. After I had epically failed in my husband's eyes, our household goods went into a storage unit and we moved in with family. I gave up trying to be the woman that I was supposed to be. I felt like a pear-shaped object being stuffed into a square hole. So many times, this is how we feel. Other people set the standard for who they think we should be and we get stuffed into shapes that we just don't fit into. Our parents want us to go to a certain college or grow up and have a certain career. Our spouses think we should be just like their parent. Our teachers expect us to become something that just is not in our makeup, etc.

All the words that others speak over us about whom they think we are or should be get plugged into our minds and we try to live up to those standards. So, many other people have expectations of our lives and we become trapped into trying to be all that they expect us to be. We must learn to release ourselves from other's expectations.

One summer our family went to a family camp and as we were doing our daily devotions I had a vision. In this vision, there was a concrete mold around me and I had shackles on my feet, wrists and neck. I had chains that were attached to an iron ball that I was dragging. I kept trying to walk, but was so bound that I could hardly move.

Every step that I forced myself to take would crack another piece of the mold. My hands were behind my torso and I kept trying to move forward. As I took a step, pieces of the mold would crack and fall to the ground. Huge, warring Angels came and drew their swords and cut off the chains and shekels that were binding me. After diligently forcing myself forward, the chains were gone and the clay mold kept breaking off and falling to the ground. I fell on my knees and looked up to see Jesus. He lifted my face and asked me to dance. Stiffly I began to move in rhythm with my Savior. At the end of the vision I was vigorously dancing freely. I believe a lot of the bondage that I was feeling was from others expectations of me. When I finally released all fear of man and completely grabbed ahold of what God expected me to be, the mold was broken, the chains and shackles fell off leaving me free, free to dance as me.

Part of learning our identity in Christ is just as simple as learning that we are- at the core-the person God created us to be. The other part is to believe in who God says we are and what we have in Him. The only way to know this is by digging into the word of God and asking God for personal scriptures to apply to our own lives.

What I have learned through this journey is that I cannot change anyone, not even me, completely. All I can do is ask God to change me.

You will be a crown of splendor in the Lord's hand, a royal diadem in the hand of your God.

Isaiah 62:3

10

TRUE LOVE

Journal

2007

As the aroma of the slow-cooking round steaks overwhelms the kitchen, promising a yummy dinner on its way, I sit at my desk thinking how truly loved I am. The girls are playing in the attic, the baby is taking a lazy little afternoon nap and my husband is working hard so my life can be so smooth. The mist off the fresh June rain fills the room and I wonder, exactly what is love? I venture to say it is something more powerful than even I can understand. When I was a child, I don't recall getting too many hugs or kisses from our parents they showed us love in other ways. I swore when I had kids I would always hug and kiss them no matter how old or big they were. I mostly got my acceptance from my baby sister. Although I had very little physical contact with her (except during our daily dose of sibling rivalry), it was her ability to see something great in me when no one else did and her willingness to think that I was more than what even I knew...

When I was in my teens I would daydream about losing my virginity. Where would I lose it and to whom? I didn't see it as something special that God had created for two people to share in their marriage. I saw it as a weapon, as a way to get love. It was something that I had and the boys wanted and that made me worth something. I thought having sex with someone would make me feel loved. That is what Hollywood portrayed would happen.

When I imagined losing my virginity it was always in a cherry orchard while the blossoms were in full bloom and slowly falling to the petal, covered grown. The sweet smell of the spring blossoms would heighten our scenes as the scene would slowly unfold. My gown and my prince would change every daydream but the scene always remained. My prince would kiss me passionately as he held the back of my head. In all of my daydreams, the prince would always hold the back of my head as he would first gently touch his lips to my forehead and then go in for that first kiss. For some reason, I thought if he would only hold the back of my head I would feel loved. Mr. Charming ended up being the musician in my guitar class. I fell in love with the way he played his guitar. I guess I thought he would hold me the same way he held his guitar but I was wrong. My cherry orchard became a party and my blossom inlaid field became a bathroom. And no, he did not hold me the way he held his guitar. I think the song he played in class lasted longer than our night together. "What have I done? Was that love? What was I thinking?" My girlfriends had been teasing me about being the last virgin in school. I was tired of being teased for being a virgin. I had Saturday school the next morning. While walking all the way to town from some farm road a few miles out, thoughts were rolling over and over in my head, "now I'm worth nothing. I have nothing to offer. Did I feel his love? What was I thinking he doesn't love me! He doesn't even know me." I felt horrible. I felt different. I felt like I entered a whole different world. Kind of along the same lines as when Eve ate the apple and then her eyes were wide open to the lies. "Was I a real woman now? Had I been truly loved last night?" This is the lie that Hollywood tells us as little girls, "Making out fills that place in your heart meant for love." This too, I found was a lie. Considering that we barely spoke to each other after our night together, compounded the reality of it all. We used each other to have that first taste of "love".

I felt my life was like a movie just waiting to be unreeled. What did I know about love? When my first real boyfriend told me that he loved me I thought, "I don't understand." Then, when he moved back to Florida, I wasn't even devastated. I thought "what is wrong with me, shouldn't I care?" After he left I felt free, free again to be me and run my own life. I missed him and I wanted desperately to go with him not because I "loved" him, but because I enjoyed being around him and his family and I wanted to get out of the small town I grew up in.

After being a half of a credit short of graduating from high school, I moved as far away from home as I could; 65 miles away was not far enough.

I was in a very depressed state in my life. It was the fall of 1994 and my family consistently irritated me with the same question. "What are you going to do with your life now that you didn't graduate from high school?" Over and over and over again, they would plague me with this question. I kept saying "Well, I want to be a singer." I remember the day I shared my dreams with a family member and she told me. "Ang, you can't do that. That is so ridiculous." Even though she was just trying to be realistic I hated hearing those dampening words. On that day I swore I would prove her wrong. I needed to think, breath, and get as far away from them as possible.

That summer I applied to a clothing design school in Long Beach, California. I worked all summer as a maid in a hotel so that I could save enough money for registration fees. They accepted me even though I was short a half a credit and told me that it didn't matter and they would get my diploma for me. So, I sent off the money that they required. My mother told me not to worry about the plane ticket because she and my stepdad had enough Alaska miles on their credit card to get my ticket. When the time came to leave for the fall semester, there was no plane ticket and no way to get to California. At the time my parents were trying to protect me but all that I knew was that I was disappointed again. I thought I had missed out on my one last chance of ever making anything of myself. Right after that, I met my two oldest daughter's father. By then I had been heartbroken so many times I decided that my heart didn't matter anymore and I ran my life by my emotions. This guy had tattoos all over his arms and one strip of long, blonde bangs that he put back in his backward baseball cap. As soon as my family met him they all freaked out. I had officially found the biggest rebel in town. I loved it until the plan backfired and I got pregnant, another failure. I felt like I was turning into someone I could not stand. Who had I become and what was I going to do now? I didn't want to hear what my family had to say anymore regarding my life. I was tired of not feeling in control of my own life. When my rebel boyfriend and I both lost our jobs, I convinced him to take me away to Florida. So he did. He went first and three months later I rode the bus down. The night before I left, on my five-day adventure on a Greyhound bus, I told my mom that I was pregnant and that I was leaving in the morning for Florida. She was extremely upset when she saw me off the next morning (I think back now and fully grieve for the way she must have felt at that moment). I, on the other hand, felt completely relieved that I was getting out of dodge. I felt my whole life was totally controlled by others and I was tired of the same old stuff. I did not even shed one tear when I left Montana. I was deeply hurt because I had to leave my baby sister but other than that I felt free. She never forgave me for leaving her and became so desperate to leave Montana that she joined the army. By the time I got to Florida, I had $45 left. My boyfriend met me at the bus station and we went straight to the store to buy groceries for the little, one-room efficiency apartment that he rented for us. After staying two nights with me, he decided that he was not ready to be a dad and moved out "OK, whatever you think," was my reply. He moved everything out of the apartment except for the chair that the previous tenant had died in. His buddy (who later became my protector) asked me if I was going to be OK. My reply, sudden but true, was "Well, I still have my cigarettes, what more could I need." Was I heartbroken? No, I honestly expected it. I guess once you keep having different things happen to your heart you just get used to it. I had learned to disregard my heart. The ones that I had loved the most did not hold it carefully so why should I. I was lead to believe that my heart was not worth taking care of or protecting.

Two weeks after Glenn (my boyfriend) moved out, he got picked up for breaking parole and went to prison. Did I care? Not really, the only thing that I was thinking about was that I didn't want my baby to have a stepdad like I had. He then asked me to marry him. I seriously did not want to have this baby out of wedlock. I know that sounds crazy considering the fact that I didn't have a problem making the baby out of wedlock. So five months pregnant in a black slip dress with big red roses imprinted upon it I married my first husband, in the jailhouse in Hillsborough County Florida. Because of the fact that he was in a holding cell waiting to be transferred to a prison, we got the one kiss and then I was dismissed. I spent my first honeymoon in a restaurant, on the beach, eating deep fried cheese sticks.

   I walked to work from the little apartment until I found a bicycle in the beach house. I then "borrowed" the bike and rode it down to the beach and found work at Ted Peters Smoked Fish House. I waited tables until my ever protruding belly got in the way of the mop. The manager noticing that I was pregnant let me go. I had made just enough tips to make rent. I slipped the rent envelope under the property manager's door hoping that he didn't notice that my husband had left me and would decide to kick me out.

        I remember the first time I got a hint of what love was. It was Mother's Day 1995. I was lying on the mat that my boyfriend had pulled in from the pool house before he had left me, in the middle of a hurricane. I remember feeling more adventuresome than afraid. My attitude was that if it was my time to die then I would. I remember feeling relieved that my family had called me from Montana (and one uncle from California) to find out if I was OK. I thought, "Wow, this is cool, they actually do care." I was laying there on my tummy with the wind howling, pieces of the roof blowing off, and rain leaking through the ceiling. As I wrote a letter to my baby's father, who had been sentenced to two years in prison. By candlelight, the simple diamond I had bought myself at a pawn shop sparkled as if it knew something I didn't. Up against my sun-kissed skin, my ring finger now had a different meaning. "I wondered what exactly this gold band meant." "What kind of future will my child and I have with this man?" Suddenly I felt something unfamiliar moving deep down inside me. It was my child; I was so overjoyed and ecstatic! My very own, all mine, finally someone who will love me for me, my Sweet, Little Ray.

    I didn't know love until I had a child. Autumn was born on a hot day in October; Friday the thirteenth to be exact. My mom had flown down from Montana to be with me. Autumn came out with her head sideways and her lips puckering up for a kiss. She was delivered by a doctor named Romeo. She was so beautiful. I never wanted to be away from her. I thought I had caught a glimpse of my mom's love for me. Mom was trying to get me to come back home. I knew that my mom loved me, but I felt that she never really accepted me for who I was. I reassured her that I was fine in Florida so a week after Autumn's birth she flew back to Montana. Three weeks later I had to take Autumn to the ER because she wouldn't stop shaking. I thought that she was having seizures.

The heart monitor that the nurses had put on her chest was not connected securely. So, every time Autumn moved too much an alarm would go off throughout the hall and a bunch of nurses would come running. The nurses put these little round plungers on her head that tore off her hair. She was black and blue from the nurses trying to stick multiple IV's in her. Seeing her that way tore my heart out. I had never felt that way before. During those two weeks, my love for Autumn multiplied by leaps and bounds. Two weeks later, a student doctor came to her room and told me that she was having seizures and would have to be on medication for the rest of her life. Three thousand miles away, my mom put my baby girl on the prayer chain at our church. Everyone on the prayer chain was praying for Autumn. The day they were going to start her on her first dose of medication, I spoke up. Before that time, I was just thinking like a naïve, young mother and didn't say anything. I told the student doctors that I was not comfortable with their decision and demanded a specialist be brought in. By the time the specialist got there, I believe God had healed Autumn. The specialist looked over her records and told the student doctors that there was nothing wrong with this child and released her from the hospital. I never knew I could love someone so much. My heart was breaking and that is how our life together began. Even though I loved her with all the love that I had, I still did not have the capacity to love others until one by one God gave me three more little humans to love. I have never loved anyone like I love my children. I was really close to a few people, but don't believe I actually loved them, except for my baby sister. My two older daughters have frequently asked me if I loved their dad. I have to truthfully tell them that I did not know how to love, then.

TRUE LOVE

So, I ask again what exactly is true love? I believe that true love is not a feeling. True love is a choice. True love means we love the other party REGARDLESS of their response. This kind of love is a rare commodity in our world today. I read a story about this kind of love. It happened when this couple had been married for most of their lives and the wife got Alzheimer and didn't even know her husband. Yet, the husband continually got dressed up, visited and loved his wife regardless of her response. Jesus says that there is no greater love than that of one who will give his life for another. Does this mean we have to die for someone else to show them how much we love them? No. This means we need to die to our selfishness and learn that to give is better than to receive.

I am still learning about this kind of love because it was foreign to me. Most of us search for the kind of love that our human flesh desires; the kind that makes us happy. The kind of love that fulfills our own desires is selfish love.

I'm really not sure that selfish love can be considered love at all. I put it into the category of being selfish. Most people enter marriage asking the question, "What can I get out of this?" Or, "How is this going to benefit me?" It's rare for two people to enter into marriage with the mindset of giving up their lives to serve one another. I had a very selfish attitude going into my second marriage. We cannot give what we do not have. If someone asks us for a million dollars are we going to write them a check when we know that money is not in the bank? Well, most of us would not.

There was a season that the Lord just taught me how to receive His love and in that time I learned how to love and appreciate myself. And in turn, I learned how to truly love others. The months after I was completely delivered from the root of fear, God slowly revealed His love to me. I could see it in the way His peace overwhelmed me and the way I felt so secure just resting in His presence. Because of His love, I desperately loved my unsaved loved ones and wanted to hold them close but could not. He gave me His love for them and I knew that if it was possible I would give up eternity just so they could have my ticket of salvation.

For I could wish that myself were cursed and cut off from Christ for the sake of my brothers, those of my own race,   *Romans 8:3*

      He showed me His love by the people He would lay on my heart to pray for. He would open my eyes to see their pain so that I could love them the way they needed to be loved. He showed me His love by the way He took care of me and my children financially and met all of our needs. He showed me His love through my friends. They were so comforting and supportive during the time of separation from my husband. God showed me His love through the smallest things. I would pray for something that we needed and, within the next few days, I would have it. He showed me His love through my husband. I would pray for God to just remove him from my heart and completely sever all forms of love in my heart for him and my empathy for him would grow. After about nine months of separation and breaking off all emotional, mental, physical, and spiritual bonds, I cried out to God, "You see my heart and you know, despite everything that James and I have been through together, I don't want to love him. But, every time I try to remove him from my heart, I end up loving him more." After everything we had been through and all the heartache and pain, I just couldn't stop loving him. Then, God would say, "Angela, this is how I love you and all of my children. I have given you My love for him." I didn't understand this kind of love. I realized it didn't matter how badly or how poorly I treated God, He was never going to stop loving me. Nothing and no one was ever going to separate me from God's love. I learned more about this kind of love through my broken marriage than anywhere else. I am so thankful that no matter how far God's children try to run away from Him or remove Him from their lives, His love can never be removed. He continues to love us.

"For I am convinced that neither death nor life, neither angels nor demons, neither the present nor the future, nor anything else in all creation, will be able to separate us from the love of God that is in Christ Jesus our Lord."

Romans 8:38-39

We all want and yearn for love and someone to love us and accept us for who we are and not judge us and condemn us for our past or the skeletons in our closets. We all have this longing to have a close intimate relationship with the one our hearts love. We were created this way. We have the heart of God and long to love and be loved. We wait for our true love to ride in and carry us away on his white horse. We all, in some way, represent "Pretty Woman." We are less than perfect women who want our prince to bring us to a place of perfect love and intimacy.

We want him to just love us no matter how defiled we have become. We want him to protect us from this big, bad world and lavish us with diamonds, fine perfumes, and gourmet chocolates. We have this deep seeded longing to be fought for. We need to know that we are worth fighting for. We want to be the one woman who holds this prince's total attention. We want him to want only us and have eyes for only us. We want to be pursued. We have this hidden desire to be asked to run away with him. We want to be given the option of a faraway land even if we choose not to go. We long for romance and adventure and we search for our hero, daily.

Why do girls love Cinderella so much? We love that story because we can relate to it. We know how it feels to be abandoned and rejected in some aspects by the ones who were sent to take care of and protect us. We know the daydreams of a beautiful life not yet lived, only to wake up to reality. We know the longing to be discovered by a courageous prince as we sit in the mud watching the carriage of family security leave us in its tracks. Our prince, Jesus, looks beyond the brokenness and the dirt. He will not accept us as those around us portray us to be. Rather, He sees beyond the darkness and looks deep into our soul. He kneels down beside us and gently sweeps His hand down our cheek and wipes away the false accusations. He reaches out and with one valiant move lifts us to solid ground. He first offers us redemption and then he offers us his world-a world filled with love, honor, and respect. He offers us all the wealth and riches in His kingdom. We are so taken by Him, we just want to rest in His presence, knowing our old life is but a vague nightmare, slowly crumbling from our conscious. We know that we are safe in this new life that He has given us and we no longer have to be afraid. We are completely transformed in His eyes with the knowledge that He sees something valuable within us. There is this longing in all of us to wake up someday and just be who we were created to be. To wake transformed into a beautiful princess. We dream of a messenger from a faraway country who will come and claim us as the rightful heir to the throne. We all want to be honored and taken care of. We all want to be safe and cherished. We all want to rise up out of the ashes and be transformed into a beautiful being, worthy of love and fine clothing. This longing is universal. Can our dreams really come true? Cinderella knew the answer.

"NO MATTER HOW YOUR HEART IS GRIEVING, IF YOU KEEP ON BELIEVING, THE DREAM THAT YOU WISH WILL COME TRUE."

CINDERELLA

We are women; beauty in every meaning of the word. Soft, vulnerable, and, yes, pleasing to the eyes of the One who formed us. To the eyes that look upon us with adoration for our true selves, we are warriors, peasants, and women who fight for what we believe in. We are women who love with no restraints. We are women with a burning passion for the lost and the desolate. We are women who long for our prince to come. We wait and watch for the day of redemption; for the day our hero rides in on his white horse and with one strong sweep, lifts us up behind him on his valiant stallion. We caress his mighty strength, ducking our head into his broad shoulders, knowing that with Him before us, who can come against us. Knowing with his drawn sword we have nothing to fear and knowing that we are His treasures who were hidden in the darkness. Knowing that He rides fearlessly, and we are safe in His arms for He never loses in battle. We wear the crown of transparency knowing that our hearts are completely exposed, yet in His presence, we are accepted just as we are. The deep, blue light of our jeweled heart beats red hot, illuminating the path for other maidens to be transformed.

    Take me away, my Prince. Take me away, my King. Allow me to recklessly abandon all others in my pursuit of You. Somewhere along this lonely road, my heart has been stolen. In a way that is pure, unadulterated I am your bride. Your love for me is a deep, blue purple-like the hottest part of a gas fire. My King, I lay my life at Your feet. I have nothing left and even my heart has been conquered by You. "As you wish," is my reply to anything You ask of me. You are my Valiant Warrior, Hero, Protector, and Light in the Darkness; the One who will never leave or forsake me and rescues me when I fall. You have taken that place in my heart that was reserved for the one who would complete me. I am undone, conquered, wrecked. There is no going back. I know that I am safer in the eye of the hurricane than in any other place in the heavens or on earth because You dance with me there. You hold me close; I don't breathe. You say go, and I say "lead," not out of obligation or any other reason except I know that You have my best interest at heart.

...for love is as strong as death, its jealousy unyielding as the grave. It burns like a blazing fire, like a mighty flame. Many waters cannot quench love; rivers cannot wash it away. If one were to give all the wealth of his house for love, it would be utterly scorned...

Song of Songs 8:6&7

Jehovah is no respecter of persons. The way He loves me, He loves you. Come drink deeply of the waters that were meant to wash the mud off of your jeweled heart. Pick up your head princess and reposition that tiara. Wear it like you were born to. If you are in the family of the King, then you are a royal princess. His seal is upon your heart. If you are reading this book, you were chosen, handpicked by your Pursuer. To proceed with your transformation, bask in the presences of the One who valiantly died for your hand.

Transformation starts in the heart. You are more than skin deep. Express your life through your defiant dance and never give up hope that you were created for a great and daring purpose.

……..All my love,

Angela

If I am to conquer the world, first I must conquer myself.

Angela B. Bowland

Revolution Virtue

Throughout the many years of writing More Than a Mud Flap, I was also raising my four beautiful children, which three out of four are girls. The hardest struggle for me as a mother was trying to teach my daughters their inner value and the importance of protecting their virtue. The most enduring times took place right before the start of a new school year when we would shop for clothing. Coming off, at times (ok, almost all the time), like an overprotective mother, my daughters and I would go rounds regarding their choices in clothing. Usually, they wanted to wear what everyone else at school was wearing. Coming from the background that I had come out of I did not want to see my precious girls dishonored and devalued the way that I had been. During those trying times, I decided in my heart that I wanted to create a solution for myself and other mothers who felt the loss of value every time their daughters put a revealing article of clothing on. I also wanted to create better choices for all daughters, everywhere. Even though two out of the three of my daughters are grown and out of my house this desire still remains and the solution;

Revolution Virtue...

Revolution Virtue-

A top quality, vintage-inspired, modest clothing line-

Revolution Virtue is the name of the clothing line that B. Virtues Incorporated is in the process of creating. When the vision for this line was first formed it started out as a modest, vintage-inspired clothing line based out of Eureka, Montana.

In the beginning, I found myself questioning, "Could anything make this world a better place or is it too late? Could a virtuous women's clothing line really flourish in an overly provocative world of fashion? Could virtue hold the torch against the giant of sexual confusion? Could there really be a fashion company that women would be respected in all of their femininity and propriety, where vulnerability would be considered a strength and not weakness?" I could see it but would it really stand a chance? Through the eyes of faith, I answered my own questions with a resounding, "Yes!" And Revolution Virtue was born. A clothing line founded on the belief that all that was once right, pure and true can be again.

At B. Virtues Incorporated our vision is to produce a women's clothing line that will promote pride in our modesty, dignity in our femininity and honor in our virtue.

We have the power to change the way the world views us as women and this starts with the choices we make on a daily basis.

Join the revolution!

Revolution Virtue coming spring of 2019!

Find us on Facebook under B. Virtues Incorporated.

B. Virtues Incorporated; changing the world one piece of clothing at a time.

Thank you!

Founder,
Angela B. Bowland

If you would like to write back with questions or comments regarding **MORE THAN A MUD FLAP** please write to:

MTAMF
C/o Kathy R. Waters
P.O. Box 494
Fortine, Mt.
59917

Kathy Waters is my mother and would be delighted to share your letters with me. Looking forward to hearing from all of you! Thank you!

Or send me an email:

morethanamudflap@gmail.com

Thank you for allowing me to share my heart and life with you.

~Angela

Made in the USA
Columbia, SC
26 November 2018